ABOUT BRUCE TEGNER

Bruce Tegner is regarded as the most experienced instructor and outstanding authority in America in the arts of unarmed self-defense. He is the son of two American Judo instructors, both of whom were Black Belt holders. His formal training, which began when he was two years old, covered all the different types of unarmed fighting —Judo, Karate, Aikido, Savate, etc.—a most unusual background in an area where specialized training was the tradition. By the time he was fifteen, Mr. Tegner was already a professional instructor and at seventeen he achieved rank of Second Black Belt in Judo, then the youngest American on record. At the age of 21, Bruce Tegner was the Judo champion of California. In Karate, Mr. Tegner holds the rank of 5th Degree Black Belt, awarded by the Japanese Society, the Shukohkai.

In addition to work at his own school, Mr. Tegner has devised a special course of instruction used by law enforcement agencies throughout the country and has been employed by the United States government to instruct border patrol personnel and Treasury agents. Movie and TV studios frequently call upon him for expert technical advice. His books are used as texts by clubs, schools and individual enthusiasts all over the world.

BRUCE TEGNER'S
COMPLETE BOOK OF
KARATE

BANTAM BOOKS · TORONTO · NEW YORK · LONDON

BRUCE TEGNER'S COMPLETE BOOK OF KARATE
A Bantam Book / published September 1966

Library of Congress Catalog Card Number: 66-23655

*This manuscript was prepared under the
supervision of Alice McGrath.*

*All rights reserved.
Copyright © 1966 by Bantam Books, Inc.
This book may not be reproduced in whole or in part, by
mimeograph or any other means, without permission
in writing*

Published simultaneously in the United States and Canada

*Bantam Books are published by Bantam Books, Inc., a subsidiary
of Grosset & Dunlap, Inc. Its trade-mark, consisting of the words
"Bantam Books" and the portrayal of a bantam, is registered in the
United States Patent Office and in other countries. Marca Registrada.
Bantam Books, Inc., 271 Madison Avenue, New York, N.Y. 10016.*

PRINTED IN THE UNITED STATES OF AMERICA

DEDICATION:

To the heroes

of the quiet battle—

those brave men who

will not fight.

GRATEFUL ACKNOWLEDGMENT
FOR GENEROUS HELP
is made to: Helen Phillips, Don Phillips
and Mike Hazy. The author wishes to thank
Richard Windishar, Herk Rossilli, Fred Olivo
and Don Harris for demonstrating with him
the techniques illustrated in the photographs.

CONTENTS

INTRODUCTION 10

LESSON PLAN 10

SOME DIFFERENCES BETWEEN SELF-DEFENSE KARATE AND
SPORT KARATE 13

CEREMONY AND TRADITION IN KARATE 14

WHAT IS THE BEST TYPE OF KARATE? 15

THE SECRETS OF KARATE 15

SENSATIONAL TRICKS OF KARATE 16

HOW TO TRAIN 16

RATE OF PROGRESS 16

TRAINING ALONE 17

SAFETY RULES FOR TRAINING 17

DEVELOPING YOUR OWN STYLE 18

BELT DEGREES AND RATINGS IN KARATE 18

ATTITUDE OF CONFIDENCE 20

WHEN TO TAKE THE OFFENSIVE 20

AN APPROACH TO TEACHING 21

HAND-CONDITIONING: AN EXPLANATION AND A WARNING 21

DISTRACTION FOR STREET DEFENSE 23

BALANCES 23

BALANCING EXERCISES 25

STRETCHING EXERCISES 26

RELAXED STRETCHING EXERCISES 26

TWO-MAN TENSION EXERCISES 27

CONTROL EXERCISES 28

FOOTWORK—GLIDING EXERCISE 29

CO-ORDINATION AND TIMING EXERCISES 30

FEINTING FOR DISTRACTION 31

BREATH CONTROL 32

KI-YA 34

CO-ORDINATION AND ACCURACY EXERCISE 37

BOOK ONE: SELF-DEFENSE TRAINING 41

NON-APPARENT FIGHTING STANCES 41

OBVIOUS FIGHTING STANCES 42

OPEN-HAND BLOW 43

HAND BLOWS—FINGER STABS 46

HAND BLOWS—"Y" OF HAND AND FIST BLOWS 47

FOREARM AND ELBOW BLOWS 49

FOOT BLOWS 50

NERVE CENTERS AND PRESSURE POINTS 52

HOW TO COPE WITH ANNOYING PERSONS 59

BASIC KARATE DEFENSES AGAINST HAND BLOWS 62

SLASHING BLOCKS AGAINST FIST ATTACK 63

DEFENSE AGAINST FIST ATTACK—SLASH-BLOCK AND HIT 65

TOE-KICK DEFENSE—LOW KICK 65

KNEE-KICK DEFENSE 66

COMBINATIONS OF BLOWS 67

FIST-FIGHTING DEFENSE: SLASH, LEAP, KICK 69

FIST-FIGHTING DEFENSE: PARRYING STRAIGHT PUNCH 69

DEFENSE AGAINST ONCOMING ATTACK 71

DEFENSE AGAINST OBVIOUS FIST ATTACK:
    DISTRACT AND KICK 73

UNBEATABLE DEFENSE: TRIPLE RESPONSE 74

DEFENSE AGAINST GANG ATTACK 75

DEFENSE AGAINST FRONT ATTACK: OVER-ARM GRAB 79

FRONT CHOKE DEFENSE 79

DEFENSE AGAINST GRAB AND FIST ATTACK 80

DEFENSE AGAINST BACK ATTACK 81

DEFENSE AGAINST WRESTLING 86

DEFENSE AGAINST CLUB OR STICK   88

WHEN TO DEFEND AGAINST AN ARMED ASSAILANT   90

GUN DEFENSE 1   91

GUN DEFENSE 2   93

GUN DEFENSE 3   95

DEFENSE AGAINST CHAIN (OR FLEXIBLE WEAPON)   96

KNIFE DEFENSE 1: VERTICAL ATTACK   96

KNIFE DEFENSE 2   97

KNIFE DEFENSE 3: HORIZONTAL ATTACK   99

BOOK TWO: SPORT KARATE   101

READY STANCES   101

FIGHTING STANCES   102

SPARRING PRACTICE STANCES   103

TECHNIQUES OF PUNCHING   104

MIDDLE-AREA KICKS   106

HIGH KICKS FOR CONDITIONING AND EXERCISE   107

PARRYING AND DODGING   108

BLOCKING AND PARRYING KICKING ATTACKS   109

DEFENSE AND COUNTERATTACK   110

PRACTICE GIVE AND TAKE   111

PREPARATION FOR CONTEST   113

INTRODUCTION TO TWO-MAN ROUTINES   114

PURPLE BELT TWO-MAN ROUTINES   114

INTRODUCTION TO THE FORMS   125

HOW TO PRACTICE FORMS   125

PURPLE BELT FORMS   126

REQUIREMENTS FOR SPORT KARATE BELT DEGREES   138

DIGEST OF RULES REGULATING KARATE CONTEST   143

THIRD BROWN BELT ROUTINES   144

THIRD BROWN BELT FORMS   150

SECOND BROWN BELT TWO-MAN ROUTINES   173

TRIPS AND THROWS   184

HOOKING TRIP   185

SWEEPING TRIP   186

STRAIGHT FOOT THROW   187

INSIDE SWEEPING FOOT THROW   188

DOWN ON KNEE BACK TRIP   188

ADVANCED BROWN BELT FORM (FIRST BROWN BELT)   189

BLACK BELT FORMS   202

INTRODUCTION

LESSON PLAN

If you wish to reach the highest proficiency in self-defense, I recommend that you follow the lesson plan of 10 sessions (below); that you have regular hours of training; and that you learn a group of techniques so well that you will never forget them. If you wish self-defense only, you need not study the sport techniques in Book 2. However, you will find them more fun than ordinary calisthenics, and they are splendid exercises for suppleness, co-ordination, and dexterity.

Before you begin actual *practice* of the techniques, you should *look* at everything in the book which you intend to learn.

The sessions outlined are in the order in which you should practice new material. Each session should begin with a review of material previously studied. When you have completed the 10 sessions as outlined, all your training will be review and selection of the techniques which you choose to make part of your permanent repertoire.

SESSION 1

Read carefully *all* the material from pages 13 to 23. This is very important preparation for proper study of the techniques. Refer to the section "Safety Rules for Training" (p. 17) from time to time.

BALANCES   23
BALANCING EXERCISES   25
NONAPPARENT FIGHTING STANCES   41
THE OPEN HAND BLOW   43
BASIC KARATE DEFENSES AGAINST HAND BLOWS   62

SESSION 2

STRETCHING EXERCISES   26
OBVIOUS FIGHTING STANCES   42
HAND BLOWS AND FIST BLOWS   47
HAND BLOWS: FINGER STABS   46
SLASHING BLOCKS AGAINST FIST ATTACK   63

SESSION 3

RELAXED STRETCHING EXERCISES   26
HAND BLOWS: "Y" OF HAND AND FIST BLOWS   47
FOREARM AND ELBOW BLOWS   49

DEFENSE AGAINST FIST ATTACK: SLASH-BLOCK AND HIT   **65**

DEFENSE AGAINST FRONT ATTACK: OVER-ARM GRAB   **79**

FRONT CHOKE DEFENSE   **79**

SESSION 4

TWO-MAN TENSION EXERCISES   **27**

FOOT BLOWS: BASIC TECHNIQUE FOR KICKING   **50**

FOOT BLOWS: BOTTOM OF THE FOOT (SHOE)   **51**

TOE-KICK DEFENSE: LOW KICK   **65**

KNEE-KICK DEFENSE   **66**

DEFENSE AGAINST GRAB AND FIST ATTACK   **65**

BACK ATTACKS: FINGER CHOKE DEFENSE   **81**

SESSION 5

CONTROL EXERCISES   **28**

NERVE CENTERS AND PRESSURE POINTS:
WHY WE LEARN THEM   **52**

FRONT UPPER BODY NERVE CENTERS AND PRESSURE POINTS   **53**

FRONT LOWER BODY NERVE CENTERS AND PRESSURE POINTS   **54**

COMBINATIONS OF BLOWS   **67**

FIST-FIGHTING DEFENSE: SLASH, LEAP, KICK   **69**

FIST-FIGHTING DEFENSE: PARRYING A STRAIGHT PUNCH   **69**

BACK ATTACK: REAR GRAB UNDER ARMS   **82**

SESSION 6

FOOTWORK: GLIDING EXERCISE   **29**

BACK OF THE UPPER BODY:
NERVE CENTERS AND PRESSURE POINTS   **56**

HOW TO COPE WITH ANNOYING PERSONS: THE LEANER   **59**

DEFENSE AGAINST ONCOMING ATTACKS: MANY TYPES   **71**

DEFENSE AGAINST BACK ATTACK: OVER-ARMS GRIP   **83**

HEAD LOCK DEFENSE   **84**

DEFENSE AGAINST CLUB OR STICK: OVERHEAD ATTACK   **88**

CLUB (OR STICK) DEFENSE: BACKHAND ATTACK   **90**

SESSION 7

CO-ORDINATION AND TIMING EXERCISES   30

HOW TO COPE WITH ANNOYING PERSONS: HAND-SQUEEZER   60

DEFENSE AGAINST OBVIOUS FIST ATTACK:
   DISTRACT AND KICK   73

THE UNBEATABLE DEFENSE: TRIPLE RESPONSE   74

WHEN TO DEFEND AGAINST AN ARMED ASSAILANT   90

KNIFE DEFENSE #1: VERTICAL ATTACK   96

SESSION 8

FEINTING FOR DISTRACTION   31

SIDE OF THE BODY NERVE CENTERS AND PRESSURE POINTS   58

HOW TO COPE WITH ANNOYING PERSONS:
   THE JOSTLER; THE SHOULDER PUNCHER   61

DEFENSE AGAINST BACK ATTACKS:
   REAR ARM CHOKE OR HEAD LOCK   85

DEFENSE AGAINST GANG ATTACK: DEFENSE #1   75

GUN DEFENSE #1   91

SESSION 9

TECHNIQUES OF BREATH CONTROL   32

THE FRONT ARM: NERVE CENTERS AND PRESSURE POINTS   57

REAR ARM: NERVE CENTERS AND PRESSURE POINTS   57

DEFENSE AGAINST WRESTLING: FULL NELSON   86

GANG ATTACK: DEFENSE #2   76

KNIFE DEFENSE #2   97

GUN DEFENSE #2   93

SESSION 10

KI-YA   34

TEST FOR KI-YA AND BREATH CONTROL   36

LOWER BACK: NERVE CENTERS AND PRESSURE POINTS   56

GANG ATTACK: DEFENSE #3   78

DEFENSE AGAINST CHAIN (OR FLEXIBLE WEAPON)   96

KNIFE DEFENSE #3: HORIZONTAL ATTACK   99

GUN DEFENSE #3   95

SOME DIFFERENCES BETWEEN SELF-DEFENSE KARATE AND SPORT KARATE

The techniques of Karate are similar whether they are being used for sport or for self-defense; the training methods and the *situations* in which each is used are quite different, however.

For self-defense, you can be *moderately* proficient in the use of some hand and foot blows, have the confidence to use them, and effectively protect yourself. In sport Karate, *perfection of technique* is everything.

An attack on the street is a fight without rules; it is ludicrous to expect people to be "sportsmanlike" in defending themselves on the street. Sport Karate is a game. It can be a rough game, it is true, but it is nevertheless a game in which the participants have agreed to compete. It has rules, regulations, and judges. On the street, your adversary means to hurt and harm you. In sport Karate, your opponent is attempting to make technical points. In contest, you choose to compete. On the street, if you cannot run, you have no choice except to fight. As my students know, I advise running whenever possible. Because there is nothing sporting about a street fight, there is no loss of honor in avoiding one, if possible. If you have tried to avoid a fight and find yourself forced to defend yourself, you are justified in hurting your adversary. In sport Karate, the rules prevent making deliberate contact. Theoretically, you can reach a high rank in sport Karate without ever having touched an opponent except to block his intended point blow.

The hand and foot blows which are most suitable for self-defense are not even permitted in sport Karate. In contest, only the high kicks are allowed; kicks below the waist do not count. For self-defense, the low kicks are most effective, and they are more easily learned. The high, spectacular contest kicks require a good deal of training; not everyone can learn them. Since contest forbids deliberate contact, the style of hand blows used in competition is relatively unimportant. For self-defense, you should learn the few hand blows which are easiest to use and most effective.

For practical, self-defense Karate, you must learn to defend against back attack and against more than one adversary—situations which do not occur in the sport.

If you wish to practice sport Karate for contest, you must train constantly and consistently, as in any competitive game. Self-defense techniques, however, are *only* efficient if they do *not* require constant practice. Once you have learned a practical technique of self-defense, it should be available to you five years from now. It is for this reason that the complicated and spectacular techniques of the unarmed arts are not practical for most people. Most people do not continue their training forever, nor do they keep themselves in contest condition forever. They need to know things which will stay with them, as does the ability to drive a car, swim, or ride a bicycle, whether or not they practice constantly. You need only *remember* a kick into the shin to use it effectively.

In their original forms, the unarmed fighting arts had no ranks, degrees, uniforms, or colored belts. They were used for the highly specialized training of warriors for combat, and the proficiency of the fighter was determined by his ability to kill and survive. Like archery and sword fighting, unarmed combat has become obsolete for war—so we have converted it to play. Having become play, it requires rules and regulations, like any game. The game is played somewhat differently in different parts of the world, but generally it is made up of three different parts: Forms, Routines, and Contest. Forms permit the individual player to practice the techniques alone. Routines are formalized exercises for two men. Contest is free-style fighting. Colored belt rankings are given on the basis of achievement in all three phases of Karate sport play.

CEREMONY AND TRADITION IN KARATE

Ceremony is our way of imparting a feeling of importance to an activity. The more important that activity is, the more elaborate the ceremony. For the essential occasions of our lives—birth, marriage, death—we have constructed formal customs which accompany the act itself. Societies differ greatly in the style and method of observing these occasions, and ceremonies vary not only from country to country, but also from generation to generation.

It is very important to remember that the ceremony is not the activity, but merely a part of the activity. A few sentences spoken by a justice of the peace constitutes an "authentic" marriage, just as much as a grand church wedding with organ music.

With the practice of Karate and Judo, imported from the Asian countries, primarily Japan, there has been an importation of Japanese ceremonial and traditional customs. Not very long ago, it was thought that Judo could not be practiced in the United States except in the "authentic" manner, that is, with much bowing to the photo of Dr. Jigaro Kano, bowing to the mat, bowing to the practice room, bowing to the United States flag and the *Japanese* flag, and bowing to the instructor. Usually, there was a Buddhist or Shinto shrine which was bowed to, as well.

"Traditional" behavior is not necessarily superior behavior. The "traditional" method of teaching Judo and Karate is needlessly rough and brutal. Hitting, kicking, or insulting a student when he makes a mistake is not the best way to help him learn. Yet, this is the "traditional" method of teaching Karate. The "traditional" method of Judo instruction is to teach a new student nothing but falling; after he learns how to fall, he is used for throwing practice

14

by the advanced students; only after months of this training is he allowed to learn to throw. No wonder Judo has not flourished in this country! Nor will Karate, unless the modern and sensible method of teaching is widely adopted.

WHAT IS THE BEST TYPE OF KARATE?

As Karate was adopted by the different Asian countries, its form was changed. Basic techniques remained the same, but in some areas there was an emphasis on certain types of kicks, in some areas there was emphasis on certain types of hand blows, in some areas there was greater or lesser emphasis on power versus speed and precision. Whether Karate is called Kempo, Okinawa-te, Kung-tu, Shito-ryu, or a dozen other names which identify stylistic differences, it is basically the same art. After all, an open hand blow remains an open hand blow whether it is called by a Japanese, Korean, or English name, and the nerve centers of the body remain the same no matter what nationality that body has. The stylistic differences in the forms of Karate are unimportant for the student of practical self-defense. There are more similarities than differences among the various styles and there is no *best* style. Since each type of Karate claims to be the only true, authentic Karate, the whole notion of "authentic" Karate is silly. Karate was exported from China, it has undergone changes wherever it has been practiced. We need not be overly concerned now about making changes which suit our time, our needs, and our place in the world.

THE SECRETS OF KARATE

For thousands of years, Karate and the other Oriental unarmed arts were practiced in secret. There was a reason for secrecy: Karate training was illegal when peasants were learning it to use against armed Samurai warriors. Though there is no longer a reason for secrecy, a sense of mystery persists. During the time when it was a forbidden art, only the exceptional man could learn it. He had to be brave and willing to risk his life, he had to spend long years in training, and he had to *keep the secret*. Around any ritual, skill, or membership available to only a few people there arises the cult of superiority. Those who are in-the-know are most pleased to be thought of as superior; they are eager to maintain the mystery—the fiction that they are plugged into some Higher Truth which gives them special skill.

Anyone who practices *any* skill for many years will develop a proficiency that inspires awe in someone who cannot do it at all. Even shorthand, a system of symbols easily understood by the average high school girl, seems an obscure and difficult language to the uninitiated—a "mystery." The basic techniques of Karate (and Judo and Aikido) are not mysterious; they are simply not well known. The ability to learn them is not related to possession of an occult gift nor the willingness to accept a Way of Life. There are physiological and

15

psychological reasons for the efficiency of Karate, and these reasons can be explained and understood by everybody. All the techniques and methods of Karate can be explained without reference to the "unexplainable." The beautiful and difficult techniques seen in tournament Karate cannot be done without long, intense, continued training—that is the secret. The student of self-defense should not confuse the spectacular with the practical. An "expert" can make anything work for him. The people who are interested in useful street defense must learn the simpler, easier techniques, which do not require intense and constant practice and training. And that is the secret of Karate for everyone.

SENSATIONAL TRICKS OF KARATE

Students who are training from books should be extremely wary of trying the spectacular feats of Karate. Many of the sensational tricks require extreme hand-conditioning to do at all. Some of them, such as breaking glass bottles, are very dangerous even when done with conditioned hands. Such exhibitions are performed by people who have devoted their entire lives to the development of such rather special skills. If you have school studies, family obligations, or even a job which requires 40 hours of your time each week, you need not entertain the thought that you will be able to acquire such fantastic abilities. In any case, it is hardly useful to you to be able to parry arrows on the wing or fight a Samurai swordsman. Keep your goals more sensible and you will enjoy the benefit of Karate training quite fully.

HOW TO TRAIN

Before you begin the actual practice of the techniques, *study* the book carefully. You should be acquainted with all the techniques before you do the physical training.

As you train, refer more than once to the written text and the photos. This is your method of correcting errors.

RATE OF PROGRESS

It is a good idea to keep a diary of your training. Keep track of the time spent on each lesson and note any difficulty you may have with particular techniques. In this way, you will have a method for checking your rate of progress.

Rate of progress is a completely individual matter. It is impossible to tell you how long it will take you to achieve a specific proficiency. It depends on your devotion, time spent, natural ability, and body style. Do not let yourself get discouraged if your progress seems slow. Slow learning is not poor learning. On the contrary, a slow learner who is conscientious may retain what he has learned even better than a fast learner.

Your training program should be realistic, and you should stick with it. It is better to practice at regular intervals for short periods of time than it is to neglect your training for weeks at a time and then try to cram it all into one long training period.

A few minutes each day spent on the breathing and co-ordination exercises will be of great benefit. Be sensible about your training program. Do not let it interfere with your normal daily work and responsibilities, or you will not get the satisfaction from it which you should.

TRAINING ALONE

If you are training alone, you will find much of value in the book. Of course, it is better if you have a partner to work with. You can learn all of the methods of striking and kicking. You can study and memorize all the nerve centers and pressure points. You can do all the co-ordination, dexterity, and power exercises. Without a partner, you will have to walk through the actual defense techniques in the manner of shadow boxing, visualizing your adversary and making the appropriate responses. Though this is obviously not as useful as practice with a partner, it is good training and should give you an advantage over an adversary who uses merely the conventional boxing or street-fighting tactics.

SAFETY RULES FOR TRAINING

Karate has been an effective method of self-defense for thousands of years. It *does* work! It is not necessary for you and your partner to *prove* the effectiveness of Karate techniques by inflicting pain on each other during your training. As a beginning driver, you would not take your car out onto the freeway during your first few lessons. As a beginning student of Karate, you are not supposed to have highly developed skills after the first few lessons. For each new technique, each partner should make his attack in slow motion. As you train, speed up your attack and defense to develop quickness of reaction. The attacking partner should not make contact blows—simulate the attack or you will hurt each other. Unnecessary roughness does not help your training. In making the defense, use only very light, touching blows. You are training for accuracy and correctness of technique with your partner. Power training is done against the bag. If you wish to practice moderate contact blows on each other, padding may be used on arms and legs to avoid unnecessary pain. (Improvise padding using turkish towels or flannel sheeting. Fasten with bandage clamps or adhesive tape—do not use pins.)

Take turns simulating the attack and defense. Do not try to trick or confuse your partner when you are trying new work. You are supposed to be helping one another to learn a new skill. As you gain proficiency, you may test each other's skill by feinting, counterattacking, or by offering greater resistance to the defense.

The general effects of this training are, for most people, extremely beneficial. If you are in normal good health, you should achieve improved muscle tone, better co-ordination, suppleness, quickness of muscle reaction, and improved breathing. If you feel extreme muscle pain, exhaustion, or any other symptom of body strain, check with a doctor. Only a doctor is qualified to diagnose your physical condition.

DEVELOPING YOUR OWN STYLE

For the highest proficiency in self-defense and sport Karate, you should learn a reasonable variety of techniques which you can perform well.

For self-defense use, it is not necessary to learn every technique offered to you in this book. If, after reasonable effort, you find that a certain technique continues to feel awkward, discard it and spend your time in perfecting the techniques that feel right for you. Each person has a different style of body action and certain habits of physical movement which make some techniques work better for him than others. Each student must make his own decisions about which techniques to discard. Remember, it is better to be able to execute a few dozen techniques quickly and competently than it is to half-know hundreds of techniques, none of which can be used easily when needed.

For sport use, students should avoid becoming the kind of contest player who learns only a few point-making techniques. Though this type of player can do these few techniques exceptionally well and can score when he has the opportunity to use them, he is a rigid player who cannot freely respond to different types of opponents. The "one-blow" player is easy to defend against by an opponent who can easily read him and anticipate his actions. The same limitation is placed on Karate contestants who have rigidly learned a stylized type of play.

A real champion does not allow himself to be frozen into the "right" way to contest. What is "right" for one player is wrong for another. Unpredictability is a great defense in any contest. If you will think about it, you will realize that champions in many competitive sports have been those who have developed a personal, unconventional style of play.

BELT DEGREES AND RATINGS IN KARATE

You can practice, enjoy, and achieve competence in Karate without ever getting a belt rating. The colored belt ratings are ordinarily given for techniques in sport Karate. Those who are only interested in self-defense Karate need not be concerned with belt ratings at all.

There are dozens of styles of Karate being practiced; each style has its own system of belt ratings. Sometimes, teachers within one system may alter the belt ratings. Thus, in one style of Karate, a green belt might signify a particular stage of training which would be indicated by a purple or yellow belt in another system. The color of the belt or any other symbol of advancement is of less importance than actual achievement. Moreover, in many parts of the world where there is an intense interest in Karate, there are, as yet, no qualified instructors to judge competence and issue belt ratings. My system of belt ratings coincides with those most widely used, but any instructor is entitled to use the belt system he approves of and is familiar with. Simply because it is different from the one outlined here, you should not infer that it is wrong or inferior.

No one can earn belt ratings without being judged by a trained instructor. No matter how well you think you know and can perform the techniques for the various belts, you cannot judge your own ability. Though you may be able to do all the work in this book, you cannot consider yourself as having a rank unless your technique has been demonstrated to someone qualified to judge it. This is not an unusual procedure. In any sport or skill in which proficiency is judged, the rating is done by an experienced person and measured in relation to the skill of other people.†

In addition to the Forms and Routines which are taught in Book 2, for each advancement in belt degrees I also require (as do most systems of Karate) winning of points in contest. Contest Karate, especially when it is for degree advancement, should be a test of skill and not an entertainment for spectators. Contact should not be permitted, and contestants who cannot play without making contact should be eliminated. As an additional safety measure, I strongly recommend that schools, clubs, and groups who are conducting contest for advancement of beginners and intermediate students should change the rules of contest.

The present rules of sport Karate reflect the original aim of Karate—warfare. They do not suit modern needs. Points are given for unopposed blows which might have been delivered to the face, throat, midsection, or kidney. That is, the players stop the intended blow within two inches of the intended target. A *token* block made by the opposing player is enough to invalidate the point. In theory, therefore, there is no need to make contact. In practice, however, contact is being made in contest Karate and is dangerous. An accidental hit at any of the allowed target areas is a hit into the most vulnerable areas of the body. Highly skilled Karate players can stop a blow with great precision. Newer players do not have such control. In the excitement of contest, they can hurt each other. When contestants of about equal ability are playing, it takes just as much skill to make a point if the target areas are shoulder, side of neck, and upper back. And, should contact be made accidentally into these striking areas, the danger of injury is greatly minimized. Even a moderate contact blow to the eyes or throat is dangerous. Every effort which safeguards the players makes more of a real sport of Karate.

---

† Most systems of Karate do not require hand-conditioning or board-breaking for belt degrees.

Specific rules of contest are made by the sponsoring club, group, or school. If your club or group plans to enter competition, always be sure to get the *rules of contest in writing* well before the contest date. You should have ample time to practice in conformance with the particular rules of the tournament.†

ATTITUDE OF CONFIDENCE

The art of Karate is thousands of years old and has worked for all those years. It can and will work for you, too. But you must *believe* that it will, and you must *behave* as though you have that belief. There are some things you can do to behave as though you have this belief, whether or not you begin by possessing inner confidence. If you can put on the *front* of confidence, you will be treated as though you have confidence, which will increase your confidence. This process is an ever-ascending spiral which you can put into motion by making the first move.

Remaining calm is the first requisite. Whether in street defense or tournament, you have a psychological advantage over your opponent when you *appear* to be calm. (If you can train yourself to inner calm, you are even more ahead of the game.) There are gestures and ways of speaking which indicate calmness. You should affect them as much as possible. For example: When others are shouting, speak softly, or speak in a loud, but controlled, manner; when everyone else is grim, smile slightly, and it will make you appear completely in charge of the situation; and always look directly into the eyes of anyone you are talking to. Develop the *habits* of outward confidence.

WHEN TO TAKE THE OFFENSIVE

It is not a contradiction to talk about "offensive" defense methods. No prudent person seeks a fight, and only a foolish one stays to fight if he can avoid it. When an attack cannot be avoided, when the attacker cannot be persuaded in any way, when you are certain beyond any reasonable doubt that you are about to be hit, move into action first! By moving first, you take the initiative away from your adversary. By moving first, you gain a psychological advantage. By moving first, you may end the fight with one blow.

In the instance of a gang attack, your only chance of success is to move first. You cannot even waste time trying to reason your way out of such a situation. You must use the valuable first instant when the gang does not expect you to act in which to hurt the leader or biggest man.

As mentioned earlier, when attack is inevitable, you gain a psychological advantage by making the first move. It is sometimes pos-

† For detailed Rules of Contest, How to Start a Club, and other advice to those who live in an area where there is no trained group leader or teacher, see *Judo and Karate Belt Degrees* (Thor Pub. Co., Los Angeles. 1963).

sible to make the first move even when an adversary has announced his intention to fight. It is not uncommon for a bully type to make this announcement to feel out his opponent. If he encounters some show of opposition, he may back down. But, if he does not back down, you can maneuver the situation to your advantage if you try to stop the attack in such a way that it is obvious that you prefer not to fight. Here is an example: In a bar, or at a party, a belligerent drunk challenges you to fight. You tell him in a loud, clear voice that you have no intention of fighting him and to move back. This some times is enough show of spirit to end the affair. However, let us say that it does not. He calls names, dares you, and otherwise behaves as though he is going to insist on fighting. Once more you tell him you do not want to fight, *but* you add, if he insists on fighting, you will fight to win. After this point, if he still does insist on fighting, you are morally the *defending* man, even if you move into action first. It goes without saying that you cannot make this work when you are being rushed by an adversary.

AN APPROACH TO TEACHING

The most popular misconception about the unarmed arts is that a holder of the black belt is automatically a teacher. Since most belt ratings are given for contest ability, this traditional assumption is quite wrong. There is a great gap between the ability to perform and the ability to teach. No one should be considered qualified to teach merely on the basis of contest ability. As a matter of fact, those qualities which are most important in producing a winner in contest are not important in producing a good teacher. In addition to earning his belt degree, a teacher should serve an apprenticeship with an experienced instructor who can train him in teaching methods.

My own method of teaching the unarmed arts, which is vastly different from the traditional one, is based on the belief that patience, kindness, understanding, and encouragement are the qualities most useful in a teacher. This is exactly opposite from the "hard" training methods still used by many teachers. Most students respond much better to patience than to anger and punishment. It is an unimaginative student, indeed, who requires kicking, slapping, and humiliation to make him learn an art which he has volunteered to study! The training methods of many Judo and Karate teachers would be more appropriate to a concentration camp than to a school. Brutality as a technique is not even approved for training dogs. It should not be used for training humans.

HAND-CONDITIONING: AN EXPLANATION AND A WARNING

Many years ago, when Karate was used in actual warfare, toughening and hardening of the hands was a necessity. Because real weapons were forbidden to them, the peasants of feudal Japan made weapons of their hands, which allowed them to break through the wooden armor of the Samurai soldiers without injury to themselves.

That was the practical necessity for hand-conditioning. Today, hand-conditioning is without purpose or function. For self-defense use of Karate, conditioned hands could be a handicap; for sport use, where contact is against the rules, they are useless.

There are a number of reasons why young men should *not* condition their hands.

1. There is a loss of dexterity which makes it difficult, or impossible, to do intricate work.

2. The appearance is a handicap to work which involves meeting and impressing people.

3. There is a danger of serious, permanent injury.

With the knowledge of how and where to strike, you do not need calluses for effective use of Karate skill. Karate is regarded with suspicion by the general public. If you have conditioned hands, the feeling is that you are spending a lot of time getting ready to fight. Then, should you need to defend yourself, you might have trouble proving that you are not the aggressor.

Since you can reach the rank of Black Belt in sport Karate without ever *touching* an opponent, and since there are so many practical reasons against having conditioned hands, I strongly recommend that the practice of hand-conditioning be limited to only those people who have extremely soft or sensitive hands and who wish to overcome such extrasensitivity.

It is true that you cannot break tiles, bricks, or glass bottles without heavily conditioned hands, but such tricks are not necessary to the study or practical use of Karate in modern times. If, after considering all the dangers of hand-conditioning, you still insist on spending your time and energy (and ruining your hands) so that you can amaze your friends with your "super-Karate power," you should do it with the full realization that there is no other reason for doing it.

For those people who have extremely soft or sensitive hands, a light or moderate conditioning program may be followed. The object would be to overcome the tenderness without developing heavy calluses. You can make a training surface by putting a towel on a table or other hard surface. Spend a few minutes each day striking with the side of the hand, using light, bouncing blows. The area you are conditioning is that part of the hand which is between the knuckle and the wrist, slightly into the palm. Avoid hitting on the bone of the little finger. After you have practiced for several weeks with the towel padding, remove the towel and hit directly onto the hard surface. Start with light blows and increase very gradually until you can hit moderately heavy blows onto the hard surface without discomfort. The length of time required in practice will vary greatly from person to person. Do not abuse your hands. If soreness develops, you are conditioning too fast.

DISTRACTION FOR STREET DEFENSE

Distraction is a physical and a psychological aid in street defense. If, for only a second, you can distract your assailant, you have a precious second in which to act. The more serious the intended attack, the more necessary it is to make use of a distraction tactic. (In sport Karate, the same tactic of confusing the opponent is used, but as feinting or faking.)

There are situations in which your distraction effort should be very subtle or slight, and there are others in which it can be bold and obvious. Subtle movements only should be used for distracting an armed assailant.

Slight distractions can be feint movements of the hand, foot, head, or eyes. Always, the movement should serve to make the adversary look away from the hand or foot you intend to use for defense. Sometimes, it is possible to distract an adversary by whispering, so that his attention is focused on trying to understand what you are saying. An assailant might even provide his own distraction by reaching or talking.

A loud yell can startle and freeze your adversary. I strongly recommend it as a superb distraction method (except against a gunman). The fear reaction to a loud, unexpected noise is one of the few instinctive reactions we have. You can use the loud yell as a built-in weapon. Trembling and loss of co-ordination are common reactions to loud, unexpected noises; with some people, the effect lasts for minutes.

Any object which you can throw to cause your assailant pain, or confuse him, will give you a great advantage and might even stop the attack. Outside, you may have sand, dirt, or rocks. Indoors, there are many objects which could be thrown for good effect. You may also have suitable items for throwing distraction in your pockets. (Do not reach into your pockets for something to throw if you are being threatened with a gun.)

The defense techniques of Karate work very well and have been proved in many, many ways. But a sensible attitude of giving yourself all the odds, should include use of distraction.

BALANCES

At best, the human body is precariously balanced. A cow has better balance, four-point balance being stronger than our two-point balance. But, we make up for our weaker balance by having greater flexibility of movement and more imagination than a cow. We must learn to give ourselves the strongest balance possible for a two-footed animal, and we must learn to take advantage of our opponent when he is in weak balance.

1. Natural stance. When we stand with our legs slightly apart, facing front, as shown, we can resist *only* from side to side. By bending our knees very slightly, it is possible to resist being pushed over if someone pushes from the side. It requires merely fingertip pressure to be pushed backward, or forward. In these directions, we have no resistance.

2. One-point balance. Even weaker than the natural stance is balance on one foot. At the instant when all weight is carried on one foot, we cannot resist even slight push or pull. We are on one-point balance every time we take a step.

3. Ordinary fighting stance. Much stronger than our natural stance is the usual boxer's foot position. With one foot forward, there is greater resistance to push or pull forward or backward.

4. "T" position. This is the best and strongest standing balance which is possible for us to assume. The foot is placed forward, and the rear foot is pointed to the side. In the "T" position, there is almost a three-point balance, because of the placement of the rear foot. The name "T" position derives from the fact that if the front foot were to slide back, the feet would form a "T."

5 **6**

BALANCING EXERCISES

5. From a standing position, bend forward from the waist as you extend both arms to the side and raise one leg behind you; hesitate in the position shown, and then continue the action by bringing the raised foot forward and bending your body slightly back.

6. Repeat several times and alternate sides.

7. From a standing position, hands on hips, place one foot on your knee, hesitate slightly, and without putting the raised foot on the ground, continue the next three movements:

8, 9, 10. Raise your foot directly in front of you, keeping your leg extended; move your foot out to the side, and then straight back. Repeat several times and alternate sides. This exercise should be done in slow motion and continued throughout your training for improvement of balance.

7 **8**

9 **10**

11

12

13   **14**

STRETCHING EXERCISES

11. From a spread leg position, and without bending your knees, bend down to touch your head to your knee **12**, first on one side and then on the other. Do not force yourself into the position. With practice, you should be able to do this easily. **13.** When you can easily touch your head to your knees on both sides, progress to the next phase. Spread your legs and keep your legs straight as you grip your ankles as shown and touch your head to the floor.

RELAXED STRETCHING EXERCISES

14. One man assumes a seated position, legs spread; his partner kneels behind him and places his hands on his back. With a *gentle*

15

16

bouncing motion, the kneeling man pushes his partner's head, first toward one knee and then the other, and then straight forward toward the floor. *Do not force.* Seated man should keep his body completely relaxed and exhale as he is being pushed forward. Repeat exercises with legs together **15.**

16. This stretching exercise is an advanced version of 14. Seated man keeps one leg extended and straight; the other leg is bent back, as shown. Kneeling man pushes with gentle, bouncing motion, first to one side, then to the front, and then to the other side. Repeat with other leg bent.

TWO-MAN TENSION EXERCISES

17. One man lies on his back, while partner kneels to his side and grips his ankles, as shown. Both take deep breath, tighten abdomen. Man on the ground raises his legs for the count of 5, while partner opposes with push downward. Relax and exhale. Repeat 5 times.

18. One man lies on his back, while partner places his hands at chest, as shown. Both take deep breath, tighten abdomen. Lying man raises his head and shoulders for the count of 5, while partner opposes by pushing down. Relax and exhale. Repeat 5 times.

One man lies on his stomach, while partner places his hands on back. Both take deep breath, tighten abdomen. Lying man raises his head and shoulders for the count of 5, while partner opposes by pushing down. Relax and exhale. Repeat 5 times.

One man lies on his stomach while partner grips his ankles. Both take deep breath, tighten abdomen. Man lying down pushes upward with his feet for the count of 5, while partner opposes with downward push. Relax and exhale. Repeat 5 times.

19. Right man stands to the side of left man. Left man extends his arms and makes fists while right man holds left man's wrists, as shown. Both take deep breath, tighten abdomen. Left man pulls toward his right side for the count of 5, while right man resists with counter-pull toward himself. Relax and exhale. Repeat 5 times.

17   **18**

Right man stands to the side of left man. Left man extends his arms and makes fists, while right man places his palms at the sides of left man's wrists. Both men take deep breath, tighten abdomen. Left man pushes toward right man for the count of 5, while right man counters with push. Relax and exhale. Repeat 5 times.

20. Right man places one foot horizontal to his partner and bends that knee slightly, placing the other foot into partner's palms, about waist height. Both take deep breath, tighten abdomen. Right man pushes straight forward with his foot for the count of 5, while left man resists with counter push. Relax and exhale. Repeat 5 times.

Same position as in 20. Left man grips right man's ankle, as shown. Both take deep breath, tighten abdomen. Right man pulls his held foot for the count of 5, while left man resists with counter-pull. Relax and exhale. Repeat 5 times.

21. Partners stand facing. Left man places the side of his hand into the palm of his partner's hand. Both take deep breath, tighten abdomen. Left man pushes hard for the count of 5, while right man resists with counter push. Relax and exhale. Repeat 5 times.

| 19 | 20 | 21 |

CONTROL EXERCISES

These exercises are mainly for sport training. In contest, no contact is made and points are given for unopposed blows which come within two inches of the target area. No contest practice should be done until partners have developed enough control to eliminate danger of making contact with forceful blows. Do not expect to have control of your blows until you have practiced.

| **22** | **23** | **24** |

22. Left man holds his hand up at about face height, to simulate target area. **23.** Right man assumes stance within hitting range and delivers full-force fist blow, stopping within two inches of partner's hand. Striking arm must be fully extended when blow is completed. Practice this type of control, alternating hands and using a variety of striking methods.

24. Kicking control exercises are done in the same manner as hand blow exercises, but partner simulating target area holds his hand at about waist height for beginning practice. As you progress in your ability to deliver high kicks, this exercise should be continued until the target area hand is held at head height. Alternate feet to develop most versatility and practice a variety of kicking methods.

FOOTWORK—Gliding Exercise

You should realize by now that a good many techniques require agility on your feet. New students are invariably more awkward in trying new foot blows than in trying new hand blows. The reason for this is obvious: In our everyday life, very little skilled work is done with our feet. Dancing and fencing are the exceptions. The foot movements used by fencers and certain dance steps which require agility are very useful in developing your skill in Karate.

The purpose of this exercise is to develop your ability to move easily and swiftly, maintaining good balance as you shift positions. It is essential for good use of Karate, whether for sport· or self-defense, that you move in for attack rapidly when you see the opportunity, and that you rapidly retreat and counter when you are being attacked. In addition to having the skill to deliver the blow, you must be in *position* to do it. Most new students are clumsy in their foot movements. This exercise will help you overcome the problem.

29

25

26

27

28

25. Assume T-stance, with left on-guard fist position. Weight is placed equally on both feet. Take step back with your right foot and place most of your weight on it, raising your left foot so that it touches the mat only lightly, and then draw your left foot back with a gliding motion.

26. To advance, step forward on the left foot, raising your rear foot so that it rests lightly on the mat. Slide your right foot forward. Practice this sliding, gliding method of changing position from side to side, as well as backward and forward. With practice, you should be able to move lightly, gracefully, and rapidly into any position.

27. When you have made some progress in the gliding action, add a punching action to the footwork, gliding and punching from position to position.

CO-ORDINATION AND TIMING EXERCISE

The purpose of this exercise is to develop responses to your partner's punching action and to improve your co-ordination.

28. Partners are seated with legs locked, as shown. Both assume the extended right fist position with left fist drawn back. In unison, partners punch forward with left fist, arm fully extended. As the punch is made, the right fist is drawn back. Use Ki-ya (see page 34) with each punch. Continue, alternating left and right punches, for 20 blows. Keep body erect and execute punches with snap and drive.

FEINTING FOR DISTRACTION

Whether for street defense or sport play, you will find the feinting or faking action very useful for drawing out your opponent, for diverting his attention from your major planned attack, and for placing him in a position which makes him more vulnerable to your planned action. (Read the Section, "Distraction for Street Defense" p. 23) for some pointers on how to use subtle hand, head, and foot movements, and even sounds, for distraction.)

This section deals with faking one kind of attack when you actually mean to use a second, more important attack. Generally speaking, you should feint or fake in opposites. If you plan a high attack as your main attack, feint a low kick. If you plan a low attack, fake a high blow. If you plan a left-hand blow, feint with the right, etc. Practice this with your partner until you develop skill in making your feinting attack seem real enough so that he responds with a defense which leaves him open for your major attack.

29, 30, 31. The right man plans a middle area kick. He fakes a high forearm blow, which the left man blocks, placing him in a position to be reached with the kick.

<table>
<tr><td align="center">29</td><td align="center">30</td><td align="center">31</td></tr>
</table>

32   **33**

32, 33. The right man plans a fist blow. He feints a kick which is blocked by the left man, putting him into range for the fist blow.

BREATH CONTROL

These exercises, which are a simple form of Yoga breathing, can be practiced for use with Ki-ya, or they can be practiced without Ki-ya. If you will practice the breathing exercises so that ⅔ breathing becomes normal for you, you can work better, feel better, and play better. The result of this method of breathing is due to its physiologic effect on your body, but it has splendid psychological effects, too.

The purpose of developing the habit of ⅔ breathing is to maintain a reserve of oxygen in the lungs at all times. Having this reserve of oxygen allows you to work harder over a longer period of time with less fatigue; it increases mental and physical efficiency, it eases tension, and it speeds recovery from fatigue.

Techniques—basic procedure

34. Stand relaxed, feet spread, as shown, fists held lightly in front.

34   **35**

35. Inhale deeply through your nose as you stretch your arms up and back, throwing your head up and back. This action opens your chest cavity wide.

36. Holding your breath, collapse your chest forward, as shown, placing your hands on your abdomen, forcing your held breath downward into the abdomen. You can tell when you have done this properly by the tension of the abdominal muscles. If you understand the physiologic action involved, you can do the breathing exercises more efficiently. Obviously, the air you breath does not leave your lungs. When we speak of "forcing the breath downward," it is the pressure of the held breath which is being moved so that the diaphragm pushes against the stomach, which presses downward against the abdomen and forces the abdominal muscles to react with tension. It is this abdominal muscle tension which gives thrust to the expelled air when you exhale. Trained public speakers and opera singers use exactly this kind of breath control to give volume and power to their voices.

It is at this point that you vary the type of control you are practicing. Exhaling through your mouth, you can exhale completely, or ⅔ of the held breath, or ½, or ⅓.

Return to the relaxed starting position.

Vary your breathing exercises by doing them from a sitting position and lying on your back. You need not do standing, sitting, and lying exercises each time. Rotate them. From a sitting position: Legs are folded, head down, arms are loose, hands on knees. From a lying position: Relax, feet slightly apart, arms loosely at your sides. From all positions: Inhale through your nose and exhale through your mouth.

⅓ Breath control. Begin breath control practice by exhaling ⅓ of the held breath. Then, for the count of 10, rapidly inhale and exhale, not allowing more than ⅓ of the held breath to be exhaled.

½ Breath control. When you can do ⅓ breath control without effort, practice ½ breath control in the same manner, allowing only ½ of the held breath to be exhaled.

Finally, practice ⅔ breath control, with the aim of making it your normal way of breathing.

Practice breath control for a few minutes each day, until, finally, this improved method of breathing becomes automatic.

36

KI-YA

Ki-ya is usually referred to as a strange power which some individuals acquire if they have an indescribable mystic connection. Stories are told of men who could stun or kill small animals with a Ki-ya shout, or stop an adversary with Ki-ya alone. Perhaps. But let us consider Ki-ya in an aspect which makes its use more practical for our purpose.

Actually, Ki-ya is the conscious use of a technique which all of us, at one time or another, have used unconsciously. It is training for the most efficient use of potential energy, and it has interesting psychological effects, as well.

Even if you have never before this moment heard of Ki-ya, you have utilized its most simple form when you tighten your abdomen for heavy pushing or lifting, and then grunt at the instant of greatest effort.

Ki-ya training can be applied to self-defense and sport Karate, and it can help you do your everyday work and play with less effort and better results.

A simplified explanation of Ki-ya is this: First, there is a conscious "readying for action" which is physical and mental; then, there is a "concentration of power," also physical and mental. The two phases of Ki-ya are the wind-up and the thrust. In the wind-up phase of Ki-ya, the preparation involves tightening the abdominal muscles and taking a deep breath. As the brain is the headquarters for mental activity, the abdomen is the headquarters for physical activity. Tightening the abdominal muscles prepares the body for a surge of power. The deep breath puts extra oxygen into the blood stream—needed for that extra expenditure of energy. Physiologically, the effects of "readying for action" excite the glands which stimulate the heart and key up the entire nervous system for special duty.

The second phase of the cycle is the unwinding or thrust. In this phase, the essential action is completed (the actual lift, throw, push, or punch) as the breath is sharply exhaled. The exhalation may be done with a loud yell, silently (only the sound of the breath exhaled is heard), or with a modified sound, such as the familiar "huh" of the work gang in folk songs. The sudden, controlled expulsion of breath adds power to the action. The sound has a two-way psychological effect. It startles and disconcerts your adversary, and it gives you courage.

You can demonstrate to yourself the effects of each part of the Ki-ya procedure.

Standing quite still, give a sudden yell. You will feel that your abdominal muscles have contracted involuntarily and that there is a surge of energy through your body.

Apply the same principle, more consciously, to a technique of punching or kicking. First, try the punch or kick without Ki-ya; then do the same action with deliberate Ki-ya wind-up and thrust. You will immediately see the difference between your ability to concentrate and deliver power with and without using Ki-ya.

In ordinary conversation with someone, give a sudden yell. It will startle, at the least, and can easily frighten someone who is not prepared for the sound. The fear of sudden, loud noises is one of the instincts with which we are born. The effects of an unexpected yell can momentarily throw out of balance all the normal physical and emotional reactions. Trembling, muscle weakness, rapid heart beat, and perhaps a cold sweat can result. These are fear reactions, and if you can induce any of them for even a very brief period, you will confuse an adversary and reduce his efficiency.

Moreover, you feel courage when you behave in a brave manner. The yell is an outward sign of determination which adds to your appearance of confidence.

Since most street fights are started by bullies who do not expect a defense from their intended victims, the yell which accompanies your Karate defense will be enormously helpful. Not only do you defend yourself (which is a surprise), but also you do it in a dashing manner which is wholly unexpected. In tournament (as in battle) loud screaming, screeching, and whooping have always been used to disconcert the opponent and instill fighting spirit into his adversary.

Any sound can be used with Ki-ya. Often the sound KI is used during the wind-up phase and the sound YA during the thrust stage. But many Karate (and Judo and Aikido) players use sounds of their own choice: hissing, ZUT, HI, or YI, or whatever suits them. You should practice both silent and sounded Ki-ya. Sounded Ki-ya should accompany all the major actions during self-defense training. Sounded Ki-ya is excellent for practicing the hand and foot blows and can be used in contest. Silent Ki-ya, or the modified HUH, should be used for practice of the Forms and Routines. Silent Ki-ya can be used for work jobs and for playing golf, tennis, and many other games. Splendid results have been reported when it is so used.

Extra power can be developed during the practice of hand and foot blows so that energy is not wasted throughout the body, but is concentrated where it is most needed. This involves a mental and physical interaction which puts the power where it does the most good. You will not be able to do this in your early training, but as you advance, you will feel increased ability to concentrate.

All of us have enormous stores of potential energy and strength which we do not even attempt to use. Fear and emotion sometimes unlock these stores of power. A mother lifts an incredible weight which is crushing her child—an "impossible" thing for her to do normally. A man remains awake for an "impossible" length of time in order to avoid death in a dangerous situation. In the rush and hysteria of a disaster, people sustain painful injuries of which they are not even aware until the excitement subsides. These are extreme examples, but all of us can do more than we realize we can. Ki-ya and breath control are training techniques for utilizing more of our hidden powers.

| 37 | 38 | 39 |

Basic procedure

37. Start from a relaxed standing position.

38. As you take a step back into the fist on-guard position, take a full breath and tighten your abdominal muscles.

39. Hesitate slightly; then punch and Ki-ya (simultaneously) with vigor.

Test for Ki-ya and breath control

Note: This is a very good test of your ability to use Ki-ya and breath control, but you must apply *common sense* to its use. It is not a test of bravery and should not be misused as such. Follow the instructions *as given*. Only light and moderate punches and kicks should be practiced. Full-force blows should only be tried when a trained instructor supervises the practice and can determine that the student has enough experience and ability to absorb such blows without pain or injury. There should be no pain felt when these exercises are done properly. If pain is felt, STOP them!

For added safety, only partners who have had some experience working out together should do this exercise.

40. Stand in a braced position; take a full breath.

41. *At your signal*, partner punches (lightly at the start) into your abdomen as you exhale and Ki-ya.

42. If and when you can withstand fist punches into the abdomen, you may proceed to practice with kicks into the abdomen. Remember

40   41

42

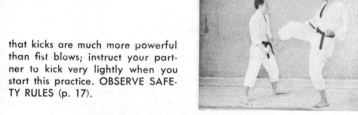

that kicks are much more powerful than fist blows; instruct your partner to kick very lightly when you start this practice. OBSERVE SAFETY RULES (p. 17).

CO-ORDINATION AND ACCURACY EXERCISE

Since you are depending on skill rather than on power for the success of the techniques which you will learn in this course, you will greatly increase your proficiency by developing accuracy, co-ordination, and balance. One way to do this is to work with a moving target. You can make one in the following way: Force a cord through the center of a solid rubber ball about 3 inches in diameter —an ice pick will usually do the job—and tie a knot to secure it. Suspend the ball where it can swing freely—a door jamb indoors, or a tree outdoors—by passing the cord through an eyelet screw so that you can vary the height of the ball.

A. Suspend the ball so that it is at your knee height. Practice kicking it, first with one foot and then with the other. In the beginning, use only a single kick in the following manner:

Stand facing the ball. Pivot on your right foot so that the side of your body is toward the ball. Lean the top part of your body back, draw your left leg up, and kick the ball with the bottom of your left foot. Immediately after kicking, place your left foot on the ground so that you regain your balance.

Repeat the kick with your right foot, this time pivoting on your

37

left foot. Alternate single kicks several times. When you can kick well in this manner, you may proceed to practice two or more kicks consecutively. In the beginning, you may have difficulty kicking the ball more than two times consecutively. You may gauge your progress by the increasing accuracy with which you can do the kicking exercises.

In a fight, no target will be as difficult to hit as the practice ball.

B, C, D. Suspend the small ball so that it is at your face height. Practice a variety of hand blows, using both hands for striking. Do not hit with force. The ball need only be swinging gently to give you adequate practice. In the beginning, you may be able to hit the ball accurately only two or three times. As you progress, you should be able to increase the number of times you can hit the target, as well as change from one type of blow to another without effort.

By continuing with a moderate amount of this practice throughout the course, you will not only learn a variety of blows and find that you can hit easily with either hand, but you will also find that your general co-ordination has improved greatly.

Most of us, even persons with a rather slight build, have enough power to hit with telling force by using the knowledge of where and how to strike to good effect.

Normally, we do not realize the amount of power we do possess, not having the opportunity to test it. Although it is more important to achieve accuracy and skill, it is wise to practice some full-power blows during the course of the training.

In the Section, "Safety Rules for Training" (p. 17), you will find directions for practicing moderately heavy blows with your partner. Full-power blows cannot be practiced for the same reason that you cannot use a friend for target practice with a loaded gun. It is too dangerous.

A heavy laundry bag or duffel bag filled with wood shavings or sawdust may be used to practice heavy blows. Suspend the bag with

B   **C**   **D**

a strong rope or chain. (The bag will exert a heavy pull, so be certain that it is well anchored.)

Using the fleshy part of the edge of your hand, hit straight out at the bag. Take a short step forward as you strike. This will put your body weight behind the blow. You can feel the difference between the force delivered in this way and one that is not by standing in a natural stance and hitting the bag without taking the step.

E, F. Hit the bag with an "edge of the hand" blow, taking a step as you hit. Follow up with a knuckle blow, using your other hand.

E   **F**

G. Hit the bag with an elbow blow, again taking a step forward as the blow is delivered.

Practice in order to develop a variety of blows which you can deliver with either hand. If you are right-handed, stress practice with your left hand to increase your skill.

G

H. Use the bag for practicing foot blows, stressing a variety of blows and alternating kicks with your right and your left foot. You must be able to strike these blows without losing your balance.

For self-defense in a street situation, low and middle-area kicks are most practical. In your practice session, you should train yourself to kick high, which will automatically give you the ability to kick low as well. Moreover, it is good practice and excellent exercise.

H

BOOK 1

SELF-DEFENSE TRAINING

NONAPPARENT FIGHTING STANCES

Whenever possible, the prudent action is to avoid a fight. However well-prepared you are to defend yourself, you gain in self-respect if you can maintain your dignity without resorting to physical violence which can be avoided. When you cannot avoid a fight, you must fight to win. In the process of trying to avoid a fight, you should make an appearance which is not aggressive. Taking an obvious fighting stance indicates that you have given up any thought of temperance and are committed to physical action. In order to shun the appearance of eagerness to fight and yet be prepared if your opponent begins an attack:

43. You stand with your feet shoulder-width apart and your knees very slightly bent. Your weight is balanced equally on both feet. Generally speaking, if you are right-handed, you will use your right hand for striking. Shown is the position of the hands if you do use the right hand for striking. Your right hand is held open, palm down. The fingers of your left hand cover the fingers of your right hand. You will be pulling back with your left hand, creating a spring tension which adds power and speed to your blow. If your opponent becomes aggressive, you may strike and yell, beginning your defense:

44. . . . with a snap blow into the throat and a kick into the shin.

43

44

41

45 **46**

45. Arms are held crossed, as shown, your fists hidden by your arms. Tension is created by pushing forward with your right fist as you pull back with your left arm.

46. If your opponent becomes aggressive, snap your right fist outward, hitting with the side of the fist, and kick into the shin.

OBVIOUS FIGHTING STANCES

When you cannot possibly avoid a fight (your adversary will not listen to reason, is drunk, inflamed with anger, or simply wants the "thrill" of fighting), then you must take an obvious fighting stance to show your willingness and ability to defend yourself and to place yourself in the strongest position of defense and counterattack.

47. Basic self-defense fighting stance. Stand in a "T" position, with your knees bent enough to give you optimum balance. One hand, at face height, is held open, for slashing and counter blows; the other is held at about waist height to block low blows and counter into the middle body.

48. If you do not wish to reveal the nature of your defense tactics (adding the element of surprise), you may assume a boxing fighting

47

stance as shown by the man on the left. The right man demonstrates a variation of the basic fighting stance by placing his weight chiefly on the rear foot of the "T" position and resting lightly on the ball of the forward foot so that he can kick easily and quickly.

OPEN-HAND BLOW

In America, the clenched fist is synonymous with fighting. This is not reasonable, but it is customary. It is much more sensible to hit with the open hand than with the fist. You can hit harder without hurting yourself by using the open hand. You can hit at a much greater number of body areas with the open hand than with the closed fist. Hitting with the open hand is unusual in a street fight; you therefore have an advantage, because you are fighting on your own terms, rather than on the attacker's.

For a smaller person defending against a larger assailant, the open-hand blow permits greater effectiveness with less power required. The open-hand blow also has the enormous advantage of safety in use. There is very little likelihood of injury to the person who properly uses open-hand blows.

Practice light edge-of-hand blows on a table top to find just the right angle for hitting. Hold your hand with the palm very slightly cupped, your fingers together and very slightly bent. Hold your thumb against the side of your hand. Use the fleshy part of the hand for striking and avoid hitting with the edge of the fingers, wrist, or finger bones. If you hit lightly on the table top, you can feel when you are striking properly. Increase the power of your trial blows until you can strike very hard on the table top without pain to your hand. You need not have conditioned your hand to be able to use this blow very effectively. The following photos of open-hand blows show only a few examples of the many uses of this most useful of all Karate blows.

The side-of-hand blow may be delivered easily in an upward, downward, diagonal, circular, or backward motion.

When practicing with your partner, barely touch the body areas. *There is* no need to inflict pain on each other to learn the techniques.

49. Strike down on the muscle at the base of the neck.

50. Strike upward under the chin.

51. Strike diagonally down on top of the nose.

52. Strike diagonally into the solar plexus.

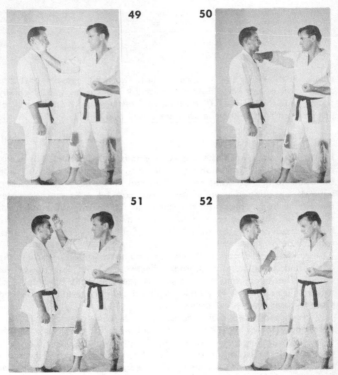

53. Striking cross-body, hit downward with the side of the hand.

54. Striking into the upper body, use the side-of-hand blow from the outside or straight down. It may seem awkward at first, but you will find that it is very useful as a counter-blow after you have blocked up and out with that hand.

55. Using a backhand motion, strike with the side of the hand into the side. You can also use the backhand open hand blow into the neck or side of the head.

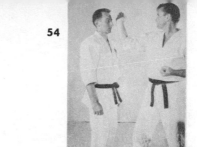

56. With the fingers curled, strike with the heel of the palm in a smashing action.

57. Hand, wrist, and arm are held firm, but not rigid. The blow is delivered with the two large knuckles, palm down. This is a straight out punch which can be delivered high or low.

58. This is a two-knuckle punch, similar to 59, where only one knuckle is extended.

59

60

61

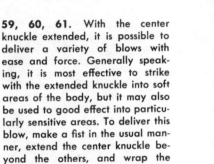

59, 60, 61. With the center knuckle extended, it is possible to deliver a variety of blows with ease and force. Generally speaking, it is most effective to strike with the extended knuckle into soft areas of the body, but it may also be used to good effect into particularly sensitive areas. To deliver this blow, make a fist in the usual manner, extend the center knuckle beyond the others, and wrap the thumb over the fingers. Striking in a straight direction will not hurt the knuckle. If you strike straight in at a hard surface, the knuckle will simply collapse into the fist without getting hurt.

HAND BLOWS—FINGER STABS

This type of blow is only practical when struck into the soft areas of the body. The advantage of poking is that it extends your reach. When using this type of blow, keep the fingers firm, but not rigid, and very slightly bent. This is a safety precaution. Should you happen to strike a hard surface, your extended fingers can collapse into a curled position.

62. With the arm held vertical, stab quickly into the soft area of the neck or throat. Other areas which are suitable targets for this type of blow will be shown in the Section, "Nerve Centers and Pressure Points."

63. With the hand held palm down, it is possible to stab straight out or downward.

64. With the palm held up, stab upward.

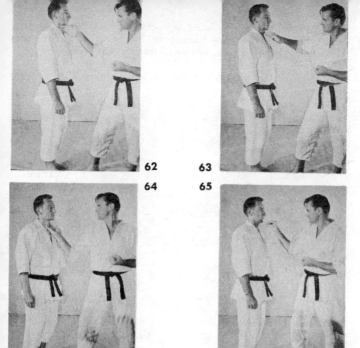

62 63

64 65

65. With the fingers bunched or held claw-fashion, you can strike with greater power than with the straight finger stab, but this blow is not as easy to use well.

HAND BLOWS—"Y" OF HAND AND FIST BLOWS

66. Using the "Y" of the hand between the extended thumb and forefinger, strike into the throat or up under the nose. These are the only two practical target areas for this blow, but it is very effective and easy to use.

66

67. With the back of the hand or back of the two large knuckles, strike with a snapping blow backwards. This is not particularly useful for self-defense training, but excellent for sport work.

68. Using the outside edge of the fist, strike with a hammer blow backhand.

67

68

69. Using the outside edge of the fist, strike a hammer blow downward.

70. Using the edge of the fist, strike back and up with a circular motion.

69 70

71. With the outside edge of the forearm, use a ramming action straight forward.

72. With the inside edge of the forearm, strike outward. This is most effectively used for blocking or parrying.

73. With the elbow, strike up or down, using a raking action. (It is not a smash forward.) This blow is ideal when used as a follow-up to another blow.

| 71 | 72 | 73 |

74. Strike in a horizontal direction. This can be either a forward or backward blow, or both if executed quickly.

75. Strike upward with a ramming action. This is a rear blow.

76. This rear blow with the elbow is delivered straight back.

74   76

77 **78**

79

FOOT BLOWS

Basic technique for kicking

For self-defense training, only the low kicks are practical. High kicks are good for exercise, suppleness, and body conditioning, but are not recommended for street defense.

The two basic types of low-area, self-defense kicks are snapping and stamping. Here you will learn the method of making these kicks. This basic method of kicking will then apply to all kicks of the same type.

Snap kicks. All snap kicks are executed in this basic fashion. When you are instructed to use a snap kick, be sure that you follow these directions.

77. Draw the kicking foot up to your knee. This is essential for good kicking blows; it is this positioning which allows you to execute the kick with proper snap and penetration power.

78. From the position shown in 77, snap forward with a whipping action and immediately recoil to the bent-knee position. You are working toward speed and precision, which are more effective than lunging into the target.

79. The same snapping type of kick can be delivered using the bottom of the foot.

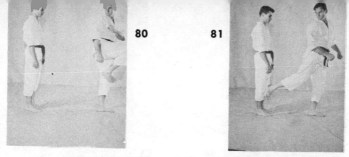

Stamping kicks are different from snapping kicks not only in the method of delivery, but in the kind of recovery made from them. If you think of the snapping kick as a whip-like kick and the stamping kick as a pounding kick, you will understand the essential difference.

In both types of kicks, you should draw your leg up for delivery of the actual blow. Instead of immediate recovery to the bent-knee position, the stamping kick has more carry-through and more smashing power behind it.

80 and **81.** Draw the knee up high and smash back with the bottom of the foot.

82 and **83.** Draw the leg up and smash down against the shin bone and down onto the instep.

   **82**   **83**

Bottom of foot (shoe)

These kicking methods are shown barefoot so that you can see exactly how the kicks are delivered. For street defense, you will most likely be wearing shoes, giving added power to your kick and protecting your foot as impact is made. The description of the kicks will be in terms of the bare foot to help you position your foot in the correct manner. For practice in making contact, kick into a padded wall area.

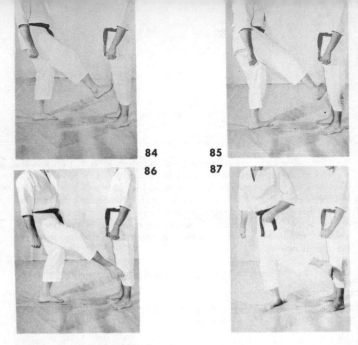

84. Kick straight forward hitting with the ball of the foot.

85. Kick with the outside edge of the foot.

86. Kick with the inside edge of the foot.

87. Kick with the bottom of the foot. Shown here is a rear kick; the same kick can be delivered forward.

NERVE CENTERS AND PRESSURE POINTS

Why we learn them

Nerve centers and pressure points are vulnerable parts of the body. A blow aimed at one of these vulnerable areas is more effective than an unaimed, wild blow which could land with force but without much effect. You do not have to learn all of these vulnerable body areas (there are many more than shown in this book), but only those which offer themselves as practical and useful. Nor are you expected to learn all the technical medical data which a thorough study of this subject would involve. Both terms—"nerve center" and "pressure point"—are mentioned here simply because they have come into common usage. A fairly accurate description of a "nerve center" is a place on the body in which there is a heavy concentration of nerves which are close to the surface and unprotected by bone or muscle. A fairly accurate description of a "pressure point" is a fragile, exposed area. There are some body areas which are both pressure points and nerve centers.

With the knowledge of how to get the most effect from your Karate blows, you are able to learn the best techniques which involve the least necessity for brutality or injury. When you know that a strong blow to the side of the neck can result in temporary unconsciousness without permanent damage to your assailant, you can avoid, for example, the needless brutality of a blow to the kidney. The use of brutality is as dangerous to you as to your opponent. It is dangerous to your character, and there is also the immediate practical danger of being held responsible for any serious injury to your adversary. Legally and morally, you are responsible for your behavior. When you can stop an attack with minimum action, there is no justification for further punishment of your assailant. When you are in danger of being killed or maimed, then you are justified in using any techniques which will save your life. This is not a particularly complicated idea and is no more difficult to think out and apply than many other serious moral problems which govern your relationship with the rest of the human race.

88A. Front upper body

1. Top of the nose. Striking at the top of the nose is very effective, because it is a painful blow and one from which bleeding results easily. A broken nose is not serious; a forceful blow on the top of the nose will cause your opponent considerable pain and impair his fighting ability. The most effective blows are an open-hand slash or a hammer blow.

2. Up, under the nose. A heavy blow to this area is commonly thought to be fatal. The misconception is that the nose bone can be driven through the brain. The fact is that the nose is primarily cartilage which is impossible to drive through solid bone. A blow here has the same effect as a blow onto the top of the nose. (With tremendous force, of course, any blow to the head can result in brain damage because of shock impact.) A slashing upward blow is most useful.

3. Up, under the jaw. This blow should not be delivered to the bony part of the jaw, but into the soft area. It is a painful blow, but not suitable for defense against a serious attack. Strike with the fingertips or extended knuckle in an upward direction.

4. Windpipe. You must avoid striking at the windpipe unless you are in serious danger. Even a light blow to the windpipe results in severe pain, gagging, choking, or vomiting. A moderate blow can result in unconsciousness and a heavy blow can be fatal.

5. Behind the collar bone. Stabbing down into the nerves behind the collar bone will result in considerable pain and may im-

mobilize the arm for a short period of time. Do *not* strike at the collar bone itself. Unless you are much more powerful than your opponent (an unlikely situation), you will only anger him without hurting him. In the old style Karate training, this is a favored blow, but it is more dramatic in the movies than practical for modern use.

6. The hollow of the throat. At close quarters, striking into the throat hollow with fingertips or extended knuckle is a dangerous blow. It should only be used when you are faced with a serious, deadly attack. A heavy blow can be fatal.

7. Below the left breast. Hard blows to the cardiac notch should be avoided unless your life is in danger. A full power kick or fist or hammer blow to this area could result in fatal heart injury.

8. Solar plexus. A blow delivered straight in at the solar plexus hits the stomach and intestines. This is not a serious blow, though it will cause pain. A blow delivered into the solar plexus in an upward direction is more serious, because it functions against the vital organs—heart, liver, and lungs. If such a blow is delivered with force, it can cause serious injury. Though it is unlikely that you will find yourself fighting an adversary smaller than yourself, you should be aware that a forceful upward blow delivered into the solar plexus of a small person can be fatal.

88B. *Front lower body*

1. Lower abdomen. A moderate blow will stun; a heavy blow or kick can cause internal injury.

2. Groin. A heavy blow into the groin can be fatal. I disagree with the commonly accepted notion that the groin is a superior target area for self-defense. A man automatically or instinctively protects his groin, even when he is not an experienced fighter. An experienced street fighter expects groin kicks and builds defenses against them.

3. Inner thigh. This is an extremely sensitive area. A light or moderate blow is very painful. A heavy blow can immobilize the leg temporarily.

4. Knee. A kick straight into the knee causes pain. If the leg is locked rigid, a straight-in kick could dislocate. Kicking at a 45 degree angle at the knee is a more effective blow. At this angle, only 60 pounds of pressure can dislocate.

5. Shin bone. The shin bone, from the knee to the ankle, is an unprotected, available, sensitive area. A light or moderate blow is very painful. A heavy blow can immobilize the leg temporarily.

6. Instep. Stamping down on top of the foot results in great pain. A heavy blow can disable.

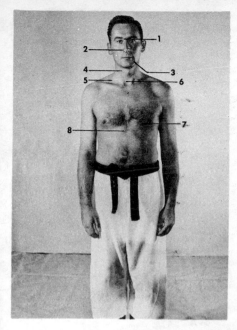

88A

88B

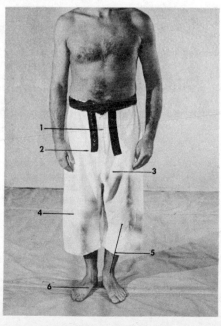

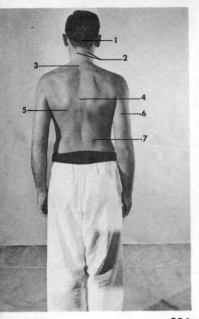 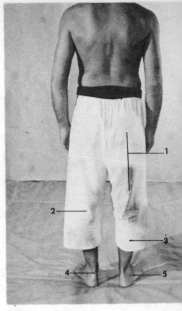

89A   **89B**

89A. *Upper back*

1. Base of the skull. Under the round bone at the base of the skull a light blow can produce whiplash. This target area should be avoided unless your life is in danger.

2. The muscles at both sides of the vertebra. A moderate blow will result in pain. A heavy blow can be dangerous.

3. Seventh vertebra. This is the large bone which protrudes. A heavy blow can dislodge the vertebra and can injure the spinal cord.

4. Between the shoulder blades. A moderate blow can shock or stun; a heavy blow could jar the heart and cause injury and possibly fatality.

5. Under the shoulder blades. Hitting in an upward direction, a moderate blow can cause considerable pain.

6. About 4'' above the elbow at the center of the arm. A moderate or heavy blow can numb the arm temporarily.

7. Kidney. A straight in blow to the kidney is very painful as is a blow just above the kidney, straight in. Hitting in an upward direction, a heavy blow to the kidney can be serious or fatal.

89B. *Lower back*

1. Back of the upper thighs. Kicking into this area causes pain and Charley horse (muscle spasm).

2. Behind the knee. Kicking into the back of the knee can buckle your opponent down, cause pain and muscle spasm.

3. Calf. Kicking into the calf causes pain and muscle spasm.

4. Tendon. Kicking into the tendon just above the heel results in pain and immobility of the foot.

5. Ankle. Kicking onto the ankle bone results in great pain.

90A. *Front arm*

1. Armpit. A moderate or heavy blow in an upward or straight-in direction can result in extreme pain.

2. Elbow. Striking into the crook of the elbow causes pain. It can also bend the arm to divert the direction of an intended blow.

3. Wrist. Striking at the wrist joint tendons weakens the hand, incapacitating it temporarily.

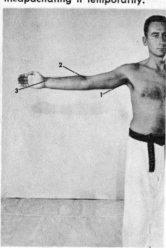 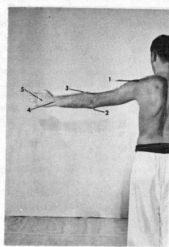

90A   90B

90B. *Rear arm*

1. At the point of the shoulder bone. A moderate blow is painful. A heavy blow can result in dislocation.

2. Elbow joint. A light blow can cause numbness. A heavy blow can dislocate the joint, especially if the arm is held rigid.

3. Forearm. A light blow about two inches down from the elbow, at the top of the forearm, can cause pain. A moderate or heavy blow at this nerve center can immobilize the arm temporarily.

4. Back of the wrist. A light or moderate blow is painful. A heavy blow can injure the bone.

5. Back of the hand. A light blow is painful. A heavy blow can injure the bones.

91. *Side of body*

1. Temple. A light blow to the temple can jar or stun your adversary, temporarily. A medium blow could render him unconscious and a full power blow could be fatal. Striking at the temple is much more serious than a blow of similar power onto the nose. In defending against serious attack, a small, weak person can hit into this area with little possibility of injury and with great effectiveness.

2. Under the ear. You can aim at the ear lobe to hit this striking point. In an upward direction, a blow to this area will cause extreme pain, but is not serious.

3. Side of the neck. This is an ideal striking area for several reasons. The side of the neck is available as a target from the front, side, and rear. It is rarely a protected area. Because of the presence of nerves and the main artery and vein, it is possible to render an adversary unconscious with a moderate blow with the edge of the hand. When an opponent is too drunk or enraged (or insane or drugged) to react to pain, he can be put out of action by stopping the flow of blood to the brain. This is much more humane than using a blow which might result in serious, permanent injury.

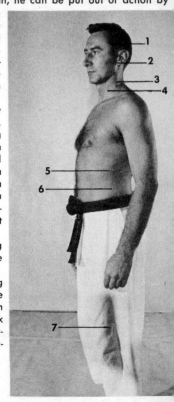

4. Vertical neck muscles. Striking with the fingertips into the muscle shown causes pain and can result in a stiff neck.

5. Spleen. A moderate blow here will result in pain. A heavy, full-force blow made by a strong person against a smaller one can be fatal. It is unlikely that you will find yourself matched against a person smaller than yourself in a self-defense situation, but you should be aware that this is a serious blow if delivered with great force.

6. Under the last rib. Hitting in an upward direction under the last rib results in pain.

7. Side of the knee. Kicking into the side of the knee or the front side of the knee can result in dislocation. Kicking into the back of the knee will break your adversary's balance and probably buckle him down.

91

The Leaner

92. The kidder, who doesn't realize or doesn't care that you find it an annoyance that he rests his (usually considerable) weight on your shoulders.

93. Dig into his solar plexus with extended knuckle. (Don't punch.)

92   **93**

94. Alternate: *place* your thumb into the hollow of his throat (just below the Adam's apple). As he leans forward, he hurts himself.

95. For the side leaner, dig your extended knuckle into the area just below his last rib.

94   **95**

The hand-squeezer

This situation does not warrant strong defense, but you must be prepared to handle it, or the annoying person will continue to humiliate you.

96. The "hearty, good-fellow" hand-squeeze.

97. Dig into the back of his hand with extended knuckle.

98. An alternate defense—place the ball of your palm at his thumb joint and squeeze it.

99. An alternate defense—place the bony part of your forearm (just above the wrist) at the top of his forearm and press or grind down.

96 97

98 99

100   101

The jostler, the shoulder-puncher

100. This man is being rough, but in a "good-natured" way. He is extremely annoying, but assumes that you enjoy his "fun" as much as he does.

101. Stamp onto his instep and *immediately* tell him you are sorry. You are pretending to be clumsy; he cannot take offense when you have apologized.

102. The same type of "good fellow" punches your shoulder, pokes you, or slaps you on the back heartily. He is not trying to hurt you.

102

103. Slash down onto the forearm nerve center.

104. Pretend extreme concern and apologize. Tell him it was a reflex action.

BASIC KARATE DEFENSES AGAINST HAND BLOWS

Karate defenses against hand blows fall into five groups. In order of effectiveness and general practicability, they are: leaping, dodging, parrying, slashing-blocking, and grabbing. (Because it is the most simple, we will begin the actual training with slashing-blocking practice.) It will be useful and important for you to reread this section before you begin practice of leaping, dodging, and parrying.

Leaping is the best possible defense—when the situation permits. On the street, you have the most to gain by getting completely out of attack range. From this safe position, you can run or counterattack.

In sport Karate, there is some limit to the use you can make of leaping. Though leaping is a safe tactic (adding to its expedience for self-defense), if used constantly, it restricts the sport player to a defensive posture. Leaping in sport Karate is best used when the opponent player makes a strong, bold, long-range attempt to score.

Dodging can be used as a separate defensive tactic, but it is generally used in conjunction with slashing, blocking, or parrying. Dodging for sport or self-defense gives you the advantage of moving your body target slightly out of range of the intended blow and leaves you in position to counter-attack quickly. Dodging is useful when there is not enough space for leaping.

Parrying, in my opinion, is superior to slashing or blocking long- and medium-range blows. A parry diverts the direction of the intended blow; *in addition*, it puts your opponent in an awkward position from which he must recover before he can continue his attack. Less power is needed to parry a heavy blow than to block it. Competent parrying requires more skill than blocking or slashing, but it is worth the effort to develop that skill for both good contest play and self-defense.

Slashing at the opponent's arm or leg is a better tactic than immobile blocking. The slashing defense is not so completely defensive as is blocking. To slash an intended blow, the player must actually seek out the opponent's attack and aggressively stop it. The blocking defense is more passive and can be seen and avoided by a quick opponent. Moreover, you absorb all the impact power of a blow when you simply block it.

Grabbing is a defense which I do not recommend for general use either in self-defense or sport. It is very difficult to grab a fist or leg in motion. After the intended blow has been stopped with a parry, slash, block, or kick, *then and only then* is it practical to grab for counterattacking. The other possible situation in which grabbing can be used is when the opponent is in an immobile stance (preparing for, but not actually attacking) and offers an easy target for a quick grab of wrist or cloth.

SLASHING BLOCKS AGAINST FIST ATTACK

Slashing blocks taught in this Section are for close-in attacks. Slashing blocks accomplish two objectives: They stop the intended blow, and they hurt the opponent's hitting arm. The slashing blocks can be used against any of the boxer's blows.

105. Right man defends throughout the series. The man on the left is in a fist-fighting stance. The defending man assumes a basic Karate fighting stance; his right hand (the blocking hand) is held open at his chest height, palm down. His left fist is held at his left side. His feet are held in the "T" position.

105

106   107

106. As the attacking partner strikes a high blow with his left fist, the defending partner slashes up and out with his right forearm.

107. As the attacking partner strikes a high blow with his right fist, the defending partner slashes up and out with his left forearm.

108   109

108. As the attacking partner strikes a low blow with his left fist, the defending partner slashes out and down with his right forearm.

109. As the attacking partner strikes a low blow down with his right fist, the defending partner slashes down and out with his left forearm.

When starting your practice of the slashing blocks, you and your partner begin by delivering blows slowly in a prearranged order. As you learn the blocks, increase the speed of the simulated attack; mix up the attacks and straighten the attacking fist blows. With practice, you will be able to react very quickly to any type of fist blow.

DEFENSE AGAINST FIST ATTACK—SLASH-BLOCK AND HIT

This is a basic element of Karate self-defense. In numerous cases of attack, it requires only this action to finish the fight: Stop the attack before it can reach you, and then quickly retaliate with an unconventional blow. The physical and psychological effects of failing to hit you and then being hit may be enough to discourage your adversary from further action.

110   111

110. Your assailant strikes out with a fist blow, close-in. Slash out against his forearm and follow the slash immediately with an open-hand blow into the side of the neck **111**.

TOE-KICK DEFENSE—LOW KICK

The toe-kick defense is a simple one. A street fighter usually kicks, and his opponent ordinarily does not have a defense against kicking. Once you have trained yourself to expect attacks which are high or low, you can easily cope with them.

112   113

112. The assailant starts his kick. This is a give-away attack; his intention is perfectly plain. As he draws his foot back to kick, draw your foot up and turn it to the side.

113. As he kicks, strike into his shin with the side of your foot. Remember, you will be wearing a shoe so the effect of your kick can be extremely painful. If one kick does not discourage your adversary, continue with kicks and hand blows until he is subdued.

KNEE-KICK DEFENSE

The knee kick is a common street attack. I do not recommend it as a defense tactic since there are many other techniques which are just as effective and which do not require you to come in so close to your opponent.

Because the leg is more powerful than the arm, I do not recommend a blocking action to stop the knee kick; rather a parrying action. It takes far less effort to deflect the direction of the kick than to stop it.

114. As you dodge, parry at the knee with the palm of the hand. If necessary, after the kick is stopped, continue with hand blows and kicks. The same defense may be used against a high toe kick. The dodging action is a very important part of this defense.

114

COMBINATIONS OF BLOWS

In those Sections concerned with how to strike, you have been taught a variety of blows. In the beginning, you must practice them singly. From this point onward, you should practice more than one blow each time. You will develop, for sport and self-defense, the habit of continuous motion, which gives you an advantage of multiple attacks or allows you to counterattack without hesitation after blocking. As you begin to combine the various blows, do not try to work quickly, but smoothly, without stopping between blows. As you progress, you will be able to work both smoothly and quickly.

When you have become fairly proficient at delivering three blows with smooth, flowing action and speed, you can add any number of blows until you can efficiently deliver your maximum.

For best proficiency and versatility, vary the types of blows so that you can react to many different kinds of situations.

115. From this palm-over-palm ready stance, strike a backhand blow as in **116.** Without a break in the flow of action, strike upward toward the throat, as in **117,** or stab with the open hand as in **118.**

115

116

117

118

119 **120**

119. From a closed fist on-guard, strike a backhand forearm blow into the middle body **120**, followed immediately by a fist blow into the upper body. These two blows are almost simultaneous; the forearm is not even withdrawn before the fist blow is delivered **121**. Immediately, using the force of the forward moving arm, deliver an elbow blow **122**.

121 **122**

FIST-FIGHTING DEFENSE: SLASH, LEAP, KICK

In this instance, you are close in to your adversary, but you do have room in which to get out of his range. There is an element of surprise in the attack, otherwise, the safest procedure would have been to leap first.

124

123

123. Adversary has made aggressive move; defending partner *(left)* slashes both arms.

124. Leap back and kick into the knee. This should hurt and distract or disable your adversary. If he is not disabled, side-step, as in **125.** Grab his arm and lock it firmly out, immobilizing it so that you can continue with kicks, as necessary **126.**

FIST-FIGHTING DEFENSE: PARRYING STRAIGHT PUNCH

This defense has the double result of stopping the intended attack and putting your adversary into an awkward, vulnerable position.

125

126

127

127. Your adversary threatens fist attack.

128. Duck your body to the side as you hit against the outside of his attacking arm. Shown here is the side of the hand parry, but you can also use the palms of the hands for this.

129. Your parry will divert the direction of his blow. If his forward motion should take him past you, as shown, you can deliver a backhanded elbow blow into his side or back.

130. Contrive to keep your adversary's back toward you, but do

128

129

130

not ever keep your back toward him. Turn to grab cloth at his collar and waist, and jerk back and down to take him to the ground.

DEFENSE AGAINST ONCOMING ATTACKS

This defense, although against a fist-fighting attack, is useful against many types of forward moving attacks. Whether your adversary is attempting to grab, punch, push, or pull, he must reach out for you. It is at the moment of his reaching out that you begin your defense. There is no point in waiting until he has completed his forward motion. You are in a much more favorable situation to defend while you are still out of range of his hands.

131. Your adversary threatens a forward moving attack.

132. *Before* you allow his fist to come within striking range, move the upper part of your body further out of his fist range and kick into the knee or shin.

131 **132**

133

135

136

134

137

133. After kicking, block both his arms with outward slashes. Block both arms whether or not he is attempting to hit with both hands. The slashing blocks will weaken his arms.

134. Continue to alternate hand and foot blows until he is visibly weakened.

135, 136. When his resistance is lowered as the result of your kicks and hand blows, grip cloth at his shoulder and spin him around so that his back is toward you. Punch into his back.

137. Kick into the back of his knees while you pull back sharply at his collar to take him down. If necessary, continue hand and foot blows until he is subdued.

DEFENSE AGAINST OBVIOUS FIST ATTACK: DISTRACT AND KICK

The technique shown here is the *single most useful and effective* defense against a fist attack of any type, and should be used when your adversary clearly intends to attack, and there is no possibility of avoiding a fight.

The technique is unconventional, easy, and aimed at an area which the fist fighter has least ability to defend; it. can be used even when you are not in top training condition or have not been practicing regularly.

The thrust and yell which precedes the kick is absolutely essential for best results. It Is the combination of these two actions which makes this technique so effective. The yell startles your adversary, the thrust creates a diversion. Note that you are not even trying to hit him with the thrusting hand, but forcing a reaction from him which allows you to begin your major action—the kick. In most instances, one kick into the knee should suffice to discourage, and take the fight out of your adversary.

138   **139**

138. Adversary assumes boxing stance, defending partner (*right*) takes Karate fighting stance of his choice.

139. To create a diversion, thrust your open hand into his face and YELL.

140. When he reacts, use side kick into knee. Continue with blows and kicks, if necessary.

140

73

141   **142**

UNBEATABLE DEFENSE: TRIPLE RESPONSE

One of the special advantages of using Karate defenses is this: street fighters and boxers are able to stop punches and kicks of a type they are familiar with; you will be using techniques which are strange to them. But, in addition, you will use not single blows, but combinations of blows, double and triple simultaneous blows. Someone accustomed to fighting on the street can quickly and easily stop a punch he expects. He will find it very difficult to stop a punch and a kick which occur at the same time. He will find it impossible to stop a *triple* combination, as shown below.

141. Starting position, both partners assume relaxed, natural stance. At the first indication of attack, defending partner *(right)* slashes both arms.

143

142. Without hesitation, slash into the neck, punch into the abdomen and kick into the shin. The three blows are simultaneous. Repeat triple action, kicking with other foot.

143. When adversary is visibly weakened or hurt, spin him around so that his back is to you. Continue to kick and punch from the rear. If necessary, you can effect a takedown.

DEFENSE AGAINST GANG ATTACK

First defense

In the face of a threatened gang attack, some type of defense *must* be made. Unlike the situation in which you are threatened by only one adversary, any attempt to avoid fighting is useless. Whereas one adversary may possibly be reasoned with, two or more function as a mindless group who can only be stopped by the same means they seek to use. Whether inspired to violence by anger or hatred, they are not moved to compassion at the sight of a helpless victim, but to further violence as the helplessness of the victim increases. The same can be said of "thrill" attacks which are motivated by nothing more than the lust for brutality. To plead "unfairness" or helplessness, then, is of no value. Whether or not you feel *brave* in the face of such threatened attack (and very few people do in that grim situation), you must behave as though you are confident of your ability to win.

144   **145**

144. You are threatened with attack by two adversaries from the front.

145. If you can, size up the two adversaries and determine which one is the "leader." If that is not obvious, then begin your defense by moving against the larger adversary. The psychological effect of choosing the larger, rather than the smaller of the two, is extremely important. Leap to the side and rear, then kick into the first assailant, yelling as you kick.

146   147

146. Kick into the second assailant.

147. Continue kicking and yelling. At the first opportunity, move behind one of the attacking men and shove him into the other man. It is best to continue your kicking until they are subdued or run. We must assume that you cannot safely run away until they are beaten.

148   149

Second defense

148. You are being held by one assailant, while another threatens attack from the front.

149. Using the holding man as a brace, kick into the front man.

150. When the front man has been hurt, kick into the shins of the holding man, as you clasp your hands and take a deep breath to release his grip.

151. Strike back with your elbow into the rear man as you strike and kick at the front man. Keep your hand and foot blows continuous; alternate between high and low blows to confuse and distract your attackers.

150   151

152. At the first opportunity, move to the outside of your adversary; shove one man into the other and continue kicking and hitting.

152

153   154

155   156

Third defense

You are threatened with attack by two assailants, one on each side of you.

153, 154, 155. Strike simultaneous blows, kicking and slashing until you can get out of your boxed-in position.

156. Shove one of your assailants into the other. Continue to kick and slash, until they are subdued.

157.   **158.**   **159.**

DEFENSE AGAINST FRONT ATTACK: OVER-ARM GRAB

157. Adversary has effected a front grab, pinning your arms.

158. Kick into his shin as you strike sharply into his side, using knuckle blows with both hands.

159. Kick and hit until his grip is broken; then retaliate with hand and foot blows, until your adversary is subdued.

FRONT CHOKE DEFENSE

160. Your adversary has effected a front choke. Strike down sharply at the nerve centers of both his forearms with simultaneous open-hand slashes.

161. Strike back with simultaneous open-hand slashes into the sides of his neck. If necessary, continue with kicks and additional hand blows.

160.   **161.**

DEFENSE AGAINST GRAB AND FIST ATTACK

Many of the techniques you are learning have a number of applications. In training, first learn the defense in a specific situation. However, although you are shown the grab as a choking grab, the same defense can be used if your adversary grips cloth or reaches out to grab you. The best time to apply the defense is, of course, before your opponent has gripped, grabbed, or choked.

162. The attacking partner, shown right, chokes with a one-hand grip and threatens to punch with his left.

163. Defending partner strikes into his opponent's right arm to break the choke and

162

163

164

164. ... without hesitation, blocks the punching arm outward as he delivers a knuckle blow to the neck.

When partners practice this defense, the forearm blows may be struck with some vigor. The contact which is made in this type of blocking may cause soreness of the arms, but is not dangerous. The retaliation blow (knuckle to neck) should be *simulated* only.

165   166

167   168

DEFENSE AGAINST BACK ATTACK

Finger choke defense

165. Adversary has gripped your throat from behind, choking with the hands.

166. Grip the little fingers of the choking hands and pull sharply outward. Grip only the little fingers, as they are easier to get hold of, easier to pull, and more vulnerable to pain than the entire hand.

167. The sharp pull is continued to one side to release the choke.

168. Maintaining the grip on one finger, kick into the leg or thigh. If necessary, continue with kicks and hand blows until adversary is subdued.

169 170

Rear grab under arms

169. Adversary has effected grab from the rear, leaving your arms free.

170. Kick back into shins, scrape down, and stamp on his foot. Do this several times, as you slash back into his thighs.

171. If his grip is not entirely broken as the result of your kicks and slashes, clasp your hands together and

172. . . . hit with your elbows from side to side into his head. Turn your head to see your target. If necessary, when his grip is broken follow with more hitting and kicking until he is subdued.

171 172

173. Adversary has effected a back grip, pinning your arms. Slash back with open-hand blows into the thighs. Kick back into shin and scrape down several times until you feel his grip somewhat loosened.

174. Clasp your hands together and take a deep breath.

173   **174**

175. Exhale quickly and drop down as you twist around to completely free yourself and prepare to deliver the next blow.

176. By keeping your hands clasped, as in 174, you are in position to deliver an elbow blow into the midsection.

175   **176**

177   178

Head lock defense

177. Adversary has effected a head lock from the front.

178. As you grip his wrist and jerk down, kick sharply into the shin and deliver a fist blow into his stomach.

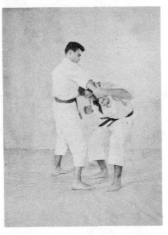

179   180

179. The continuous action of kicking and striking will allow you to release your head. Maintain your grip on his wrist.

180. If necessary, continue with a forceful heel-of-the-palm blow up under the chin.

181   182

Rear-arm choke or head lock

181. Adversary has effected a rear choke with the forearm.

182. Grip the choking arm at wrist and elbow as you turn your head into the crook of his elbow to relieve some of the throat pressure. As you grip, jerk down on his arm and kick back into the shin.

183. The simultaneous actions of jerking and kicking should release his grip sufficiently to allow you to turn half-way around and begin to pull your head out of his grip. If the first kick back does not accomplish the needed release, kick several times.

184. Maintaining the grip on his wrist, continue to step back and pull your head completely out of the grip. Continue kicking, if necessary.

183   184

185   186

185. Finish in close, with hand blows to the body, or

186. . . . pull his arm behind him, striking into the rear body. For a takedown, kick into the back of his leg at the knee.

Note: The defense used against a head lock is exactly the same from 183 to finish. To effect release, remember to kick and stamp.

DEFENSE AGAINST WRESTLING: FULL NELSON

187. Adversary has effected a full nelson.

188. Relieve pressure by gripping your hands as shown and pressing back against your forehead.

189. Close-up of action to relieve pressure and pain.

187   188   189

190   **191**

192   **193**

190. Kick sharply into the shin, several times.

191. When his grip is somewhat loosened as the result of your kicks, step back with your left foot between (and in back of) his feet, strike into the back of his knee with your knee, and grip his trousers with your left hand.

192. Twist him back over your thigh, pull with your left hand so that he is lifted up and back, and place him on the ground.

193. Prepare to continue kicking and hand blows if he is not subdued.

194. Adversary threatens overhead club attack.

195. Because the club (or stick) is an extension of the arm, move in under and beyond the weapon for safety. This is one of the very few instances in which moving *into* the adversary is recommended. Block the threatening arm with crossed forearms, taking a deep step forward as you block.

194   195

196. Grip his wrist with your right hand and jerk him forward off balance.

197. Smash down with your forearm against his elbows as you continue to pull on his wrist. Maintaining your grip on his wrist, you can continue, if necessary, with foot blows into legs and head.

196   197

198   **199**

Side swing attack

198. Adversary threatens club attack, swinging the weapon from the side.

199. Step in past the range of the club as you block his attacking arm with your open hands (or forearms).

200   **201**

200. Grip cloth at his sleeve and pull forward to capture his arm as you deliver a heel of the palm blow sharply up under his chin.

201. Place your leg behind him, continue to clamp his captured arm into your side and take him down by delivering a second vigorous palm of the hand blow.

202   **203**

Backhand attack

202. Your adversary threatens to attack with a backhand blow.

203. Take a step in and block his striking arm with both your forearms.

204. Grip his wrist with your right hand and pull his arm back and up as you deliver a sharp blow with your forearm against his elbow. If necessary, continue with foot blows until he is subdued. Do not attempt to take the club from him until he is visibly weakened.

204

WHEN TO DEFEND AGAINST AN ARMED ASSAILANT

In *any* situation, no matter how well trained you are, it is best to avoid fighting by either running away or talking your way out. In the case of a threatened attack with a weapon, it is even *more* important to avoid fighting, *if you can.*

Armed attacks which are unprovoked, unpremeditated, and entirely without motive are statistically very rare. We read about them in the paper because they are so dramatic and *because* they are unusual. Since most armed attacks have some purpose, it is extremely important that you evaluate the situation before rushing into action.

Robbery is the most common motive for gun attack. The gun is intended to persuade; the gunman actually prefers not to use his weapon. The wisest, safest, most logical behavior is to give up your money and offer no resistance. To the contrary, you can further assure your safety by making it clear to the robber that you do not intend to endanger your life by fighting for money. This reassurance is particularly useful if you are faced with a nervous or nonprofessional robber.

If robbery is not the motive for gun attack (remember that completely unmotivated gun attack is rare), then you may even know your assailant and decide whether or not you can reason with him (or her). If the person holding the gun actually intends to kill you, then you must go into action with the appropriate defense.

Cutting weapons are sometimes used as threat for robbery, in which case you follow the same procedure as with gun attack—lose your money, save your life. In the case of cutting weapon attacks, when the assailant is not threatening but really intends to kill or injure you, your best chance of survival is to go into action immediately, unless you can run away.

Distraction, useful for all defense techniques, is *essential* with defenses against armed attack. Reread "Distraction for Street Defense" (p. 23). Remember that only the slight and subtle distractions are suitable. An obvious distraction may frighten a nervous or amateur gunman and make the situation worse.

FIRST GUN DEFENSE
Reread the introduction to weapons defenses (p. 90).

205. Your adversary threatens you with a gun from the front, close in.

206. PROVIDED THE SITUATION CALLS FOR DEFENSE, distract his attention (see "Distraction for Street Defense," p. 23).

205   **206**

207 **208**

209 **210**

207. When his attention is diverted, grab his gun hand and push it to deflect the barrel from you. Grip his hand and gun in such a manner that the action is locked. If there is great likelihood of being threatened with gun attack, learn some basic information about guns so that you understand how they fire and what prevents firing.

208. Maintaining your grip on his hand, stab into the face. (This is one of the few situations in which stabbing into the eyes is justified.)

209. Kick into the legs or lower body with force as you grip the gun hand with your right hand.

210. When your adversary has been visibly weakened as the result of your kicks, pivot clockwise, sliding your left forearm over his forearm. Maintain your grip on his hand.

211   **212**

211. Pull up and back on his held hand, twisting his wrist as you pull.

212. If you lower your body as you twist and pull, you can take him down to the ground. Do not release your grip on his hand until you have taken the weapon from him.

SECOND GUN DEFENSE
Reread the introduction to weapons defenses (p. 90).

213. Adversary threatens with gun held at his side. PROVIDED THE SITUATION IS APPROPRIATE, distract his attention. In the photo shown, the assailant has been asked to get something out of the defending partner's pocket or wallet.

214. While the adversary is engaged in reaching out, grip his gun hand and deflect the barrel from you, locking the action.

213   **214**

215

216

215. Stab into the throat or face.

216. Kick into the shins and grip the gun hand with both your hands to prevent firing of the gun. This is usually sufficient to subdue. If necessary, you can complete the defense by following through.

217, 218. Keeping the muzzle pointed away from you continually, step in, twist the gun hand, and strike into your adversary's ribs with your elbow.

219. Maintain your grip with your left hand and step around in back of him, twisting his arm up his back. From this position, you can control him and walk him away.

217

218

219

220	**221**	**222**

THIRD GUN DEFENSE

Reread the introduction to weapons defenses (p. 90).

220. You are threatened by gun held to your back. If the situation warrants defense, distract your adversary's attention by hand or head motion or in any of the ways suggested to you in the Section, "Distraction for Street Defense." Do not make your next move until you have determined which hand holds the gun.

221. When his attention is diverted, turn in the direction of the gun hand and hit back with your forearm.

222. Complete your turn, as you stab into the face or eyes, sliding his gun hand along your upper arm and

223. . . . lock his wrist into the crook of your elbow as you step around in back of him. The left arm hits against the side of his head.

224. Pull back with your right arm, push with your left arm, and kick with your knee into the back of his knee. Do not release him until he has let go of his weapon.

223	**224**

DEFENSE AGAINST CHAIN (OR FLEXIBLE WEAPON)

Your best defense against flexible weapons, when it is absolute impossible for you to run away (the most sensible action), is to lea out of range.

225. Adversary attacks with chain (rope, hose, or any flexib weapon). At the first sign of attack, leap back out of range ar allow the chain to swing past you.

226. Only when the chain has gone past you, and before yo adversary makes a second attempt, kick at his legs and move arour to his rear, making further retalitatory blows from the rear.

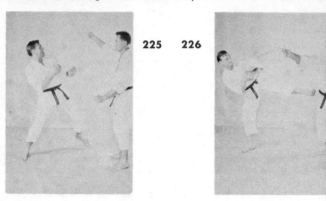

225   226

FIRST KNIFE DEFENSE: VERTICAL ATTACK

227, 228, 229. When your adversary is attacking in the mann shown in any of the photos, the defense is made in terms of th *direction* of the attack, not of the *style* of attack. With the knife mo ing straight in, the defense is the same for all three styles.

227   **228**   **229**

230. Leap to the side of the attacking knife hand. The ideal direction for your leap is at a 45 degree angle to the side, and somewhat to the rear, of the adversary. You are then in a relatively safe position in relation to his attacking hand.

231. Before he has a chance to turn and face your new position, kick forcefully into his leg, aiming for the back of his knee to push him off balance.

232. Continue to kick until he is subdued. Do not attempt to get in close enough to grapple or deliver hand blows until he is visibly weakened.

230   231   232

Note: Exactly the same defense can be used if your adversary is attacking with a broken bottle, can opener, or any cutting weapon.

SECOND KNIFE DEFENSE
This is the type of attack ordinarily made by someone experienced in the use of knives. Rather than making an obvious attack, this opponent will generally stalk his intended victim, crouching, waiting for a move which gives him an easy target. Before making any move of defense, you *must distract* him to give you the opening you need.

233   **234**

233. Adversary threatens knife attack without revealing the direction or style he intends to use.

234. *Distract.* Shown here is a slight hand movement. See the Section, "Distraction for Street Defense," for further material on this important subject.

235   **236**

235. When his eyes are on your moving hand, kick the outside of his wrist.

236. Follow the first kick immediately with a second kick into his leg.

237   **238**   **239**

237, 238. Move to the rear of your adversary and continue to kick and slash until he is visibly weakened.

239. Only when he is visibly weakened, grip the knife hand (at the wrist) and smash down at the back of his elbow with a forearm blow. If necessary, continue kicking and hitting until he is completely subdued.

THIRD KNIFE DEFENSE: HORIZONTAL ATTACK

The direction in which the knife is moving determines the appropriate defense. No matter what style of attack is being used, this defense is used when the knife is being swung in a horizontal direction. Though the leap to the side and back is safest for the straight-in attack, it cannot be used here because the weapon threatens in an arc of 180 degrees.

240. The horizontal attack is obvious from the way your adversary swings the knife.

241. Leap straight back, out of range.

240   **241**

242. When the knife hand of your adversary is in the least dangerous position, kick into his legs.

243. After the first kick, leap to his side or to his rear and continue kicking until he is subdued. When he is visibly weakened, slash his arms. Continue hand and foot blows from the rear of your adversary until he is subdued.

242

243

BOOK 2

SPORT KARATE

READY STANCES

The following are the basic ready stances for sport Karate. There is no application of these ready stances to self-defense situations. They have become part of the ritual of practicing sport Karate.

244. Basic ready stance. Feet are shoulder-width apart, weight is placed equally on both feet, knees are slightly bent, body is erect. Fists are held firmly at upper thigh, palms in.

245. Covered fist ready stance. Body and feet are held as in the Basic Ready Stance. The right fist is held at face height and is covered by the left hand.

246. Fists at hips ready stance. Body and feet are held as in the Basic Ready Stance. Fists are held at the hips, palms up.

247. Body and feet are held as in the Basic Ready Stance. Hands are held palms out.

244   245   246   247

248. "T" ready stance. Fists are held at the right hip, palm over palm; the left foot is forward. Feet are in a wide "T" position, body erect.

FIGHTING STANCES

249. Fist and open-hand fighting stance. Feet are placed in a "T" position, body erect. Left hand is held open, palm down at shoulder height. Right fist is held palm up at waist height.

250. Open-hand on-guard stance. Body erect, feet in "T" position. Left open hand is held forward at about face height, palm in; right open hand is held at the midsection, palm up.

251. Fist on-guard stance. Feet are placed in "T" position, body erect. One fist is held at face height, forward; the other fist is placed palm up at the hip.

249   250   251   252

252. Overhead slashing on-guard stance. Most of the body weight is placed on the rear foot, and the front foot is used as a balance. The front foot can kick easily from this stance without loss of balance. Right hand is held palm out above the head, and the left hand is held forward in a slashing position.

253   **254**   **255**

Fighting stances are a matter of choice and personal style. Your fighting stance can be your favored attacking stance, or you can assume a stance in response to your opponent player's.

253.   Low blocking stance. The weight of the body is carried mainly by the forward foot. One fist is held low to block low attacks; and the other fist is held at the hip.

254.   Switching open-hand stance. This is a versatile, flexible stance useful for drawing out the opponent player's strategy. Feet are placed wide apart with weight equally divided. Shown here, the player has positioned himself so that he can easily move 90 degrees from side to side without loss of balance. As he waits out his opponent's move, he switches his hands, first one hand high and then the other.

255.   Kick or stab stance. Most of the body weight is carried on the rear foot, with the ball of the forward foot used for balance. Both hands are held in a stabbing position. It is possible to kick or stab very quickly from this stance.

SPARRING PRACTICE STANCES

Though highly impractical for modern street defense, the fighting stances of contest Karate must be learned by the student interested in Karate for sport.

For Karate contest, the student should learn a variety of stances, so that he can cope with different kinds of competition. He should learn stances for defensive and offensive play. He should know stances to deal with players who favor high attacks as well as those who attack low. He should know stances for players who prefer hand and fist attacks and for those who favor kicking techniques.

256. Left player is in a cat-claw-ing stance; right player is in a "T" stance with vertical guard.

258

257. Left player is in cat-clawing stance, leading with right hand; right player is in stork stance with horizontal guard.

258. Left player is in cat stance with overhead, palm-out guard; right player is in "T" stance with stabbing guard.

TECHNIQUES OF PUNCHING

The aim in sport training is perfection of technique. In this one important element, sport training differs greatly from self-defense training. In a defensive situation on the street, there is no judge to give you points for beauty of technique. In sport contest, good form can determine whether you win or lose a match.

259, 260, 261. These three photos show *one* action carried through from start to finish. In this practice, the right man is simply your

259   260

reference target. You may practice this kind of technique without an actual target, or against a sandbag or padded wall area. Note that the right fist starts the punch with palm up. As the punch is half-way to the target (260), the fist has turned over half-way. The fist maintains this half-way position and makes the complete turn as shown in 261 at the instant of simulated impact. As the punching fist snaps up, the other fist is snapped back to create a reciprocal force to give more power to the punching fist. This snapping back of the nonpunching fist adds another body action, that of shoulder twist, torquing more power into the blow. Your practice of this action is necessary for timing, precision, and speed.

259, 262, 263. The action in this series is similar to that in 259, 260, 261, but the punch has a hooking action (presumably because your opponent has a front guard up).

259, 264. This is not a widely used sport blow, but it is a good idea to practice the less common blows and develop a style of fighting which is not predictable and which makes defense more difficult for the opposing player.

In this upper blow, the fist does not turn over, but the nonpunching fist snaps back with even greater vigor to add torque.

The shifting of body weight in all these blows is minor. Leaning into the blow is not necessary when torque, speed, and precision are achieved.

MIDDLE-AREA KICKS

For sport training, you will be required to use middle-area and high kicks only. This type of kick is not advised for street defense, but makes excellent body-conditioning practice. If you train yourself to kick well at the middle and high areas, you will find the low-area, self-defense kicks very simple to execute.

The three kicks which are basic to sport Karate are the side snap, front stamp, and circle (or hooking) kicks. These are the most efficient kicks which you will need for sport training.

265. The side-snap kick should be practiced first from a standing position, with the kicking foot drawn up to the knee, as shown.

266. Deliver the side-snap kick with the leg fully extended; the thrust is horizontal. Recover to the position in 265, and then place the kicking foot down. This type of practice will improve your balance.

267. First, the leg is drawn up with the knee as close to the body as you can get it, and the kick delivered with a stamping action straight out. Recover into the bent-knee position before placing the kicking foot down on the floor.

265 266
267 268

269　　　　**270**

268, 269.   Draw the kicking leg up and back, delivering the blow in a circular direction. The blow is delivered with the ball of the foot, toes curled for safety. Recover first to the position in 268 and then place the kicking foot down.

HIGH KICKS FOR CONDITIONING AND EXERCISE

These kicks have no practical application for self-defense and very little for sport. They are offered only as a training procedure. By practicing kicking higher than necessary, you will increase the suppleness and agility of your legs and greatly improve body balance.

270.   This is a swinging high kick. First, draw your knee as close to your body as you can get it; then swing upward as you reach as high as you can with your foot. Keep your body erect and maintain balance.

271.   Bending your knee only slightly, swing your leg in an arc in both directions past your target. Maintain balance.

272.   With the toes pointed down, kick up with the knee as high as possible, keeping your body as erect as you can.

The man on the left is shown simply as a reference target. You may practice this without a partner, always using both legs, alternately.

271　　　　**272**

273. The attack is similar in all four photos. It is a straight punch. The first defense is a forearm parry, hitting the opponent's forearm from the outside.

274. The heel of the palm is used to parry. While the forearm parry is easier to execute, the heel-of-the-palm parry can be done from a greater distance.

273   **274**

275. The punch is stopped with a two-handed parry, which gives added power and moves the opponent into an awkward, vulnerable position.

276. Without moving his feet, the defending partner avoids a punch by leaning his upper body out of fist range. Obviously, this must be done quickly. Counterattack is now possible. Dodging out to the side is also possible.

275   **276**

277   **278**

BLOCKING AND PARRYING KICKING ATTACKS

Self-defense and sport training differ in very important aspects. As you train for these particular sport techniques, do not confuse them with practical street defense. In contest or tournament, your opponent's kick may be *technically* nullified if your parry or block is merely a token resistance. A point blow is one which is altogether unopposed. On the street, a token resistance to a kicking attack would not be sufficient to stop the kick, because the leg is so much more powerful than the arm.

277.   A side-snap kick is blocked with a horizontal forearm.

278.   A forward thrusting kick is parried with an inner forearm blow.

279.   A forward thrusting kick is parried with the palm of the hand.

280.   A side-snap kick is parried with a backhand blow using the outside of the forearm.

281.   A high kick is parried with a two-handed heel of the palm blow.

279   **280**   **281**

DEFENSE AND COUNTERATTACK

This is your beginning practice for combining defense and counterattack. Throughout your training you must keep this in mind: Specific combinations of defense and attack are shown in the photos and explained in the text. If you wish to develop versatility and style, you must immediately start experimenting with combinations different from the ones shown. Though you may have learned only a few techniques, combine those few techniques in a variety of ways. As you learn more techniques, your variations will become more interesting, and your personal style will develop. Unless you start in this manner, you will become rigid in the use of the techniques you know. It is, of course, very important to know how to execute the separate techniques well, but you should also train your mind to combine them flexibly and spontaneously.

282, 283. Left partner attacks throughout. A high fist blow is slashed or blocked with a vertical forearm blow. The counterattack is a middle-body straight punch.

284, 285. A high open-hand blow is stopped with an outward forearm slash or block; the counterattack is a side-snap kick.

282   283

284   285

110

286   287

PRACTICE OF GIVE AND TAKE

Hand blows

Practice with smooth, flowing action. Only one attack is made each time. For each attack, the defending partner first defends, then attacks. There is no prearrangement of types of hand blows; partners should start out by practicing fairly slowly. As proficiency increases, speed of attack and defense can increase until practice of this kind is very rapid. Contact is not made except to block.

286. Left man punches with a high fist blow which is slashed by the right man, who then counters with a stab to the upper body **287**.

Without interruption of rhythm, the partners withdraw very slightly to position themselves for the next attack-defense.

288. Right man attacks with a right fist blow which is parried by the left man, who then counters with an elbow blow into the middle body **289**.

288   289

290 **291**

Attack, defense, and counterattack

290. Both men are in sparring fighting stances of their choice.

291. Left man punches as right man blocks up with his forearm.

292 **293**

292, 293. Right man counters with a side snap kick high, causing his opponent to dodge, allowing for a further attack with a fist blow **294.**

These are only a few examples of the kinds of attack-defense-counterattack which you must practice. Use all the blows you have learned and reverse the attacker-defender roles so that both partners can get practice in defending and attacking.

294   **295**

PREPARATION FOR CONTEST

295. Starting position. Both players face each other in a Position of Attention. Shown here, the men are closer together than they should be for start of an actual contest. The commonly used spacing is 12 feet apart.

296. At a signal, the players bow to the referee (or instructor) and then to each other. The bow is the formal gesture of respect common to most sport games and is similar to the crossed foils in fencing and the handshake of many combat sports.

297. After the bow, the players remain in a Position of Attention until the signal is given for contest to begin. At the signal to begin, the players assume the fighting stances of their choice.

296   **297**

INTRODUCTION TO TWO-MAN ROUTINES

The purpose of these prearranged two-man routines is to practice for speed, precision, and body-conditioning. This method of practice is rigid and must be alternated with more flexible ones to develop strong proficiency. Practice of routines accomplishes much the same results as calisthenics, but are more interesting to do.

At the beginning of your practice of the two-man routines, work slowly to avoid making contact. As you progress, the blows should be delivered with all the force of an actual blow, though they must not come closer than *two inches* to the target. Finally, when practicing the routines properly, the partners should move slowly and deliberately into position for the attack-defense-counter-attack, and then the blows and blocks should be fast, powerful, and controlled. Except for blocking, *contact is never made.*

For the purpose of exercise and conditioning, the routines may be practiced without attempting perfection of technique. If the student is working for a belt rating, the demonstration of the routines must show technical excellence.

PURPLE BELT TWO-MAN ROUTINES

First routine

298. All two-man routines begin with partners standing about 4 feet apart, fists held loosely at sides.

299. Partners bow in unison.

300. Partners return to starting position.

301. Left partner assumes palm-over-fist ready stance as right partner steps back with right foot, assuming a fighting stance.

302. Right partner steps forward with right foot as he punches straight out with right fist, drawing left fist to side. As the punch is made, left partner steps to left with left foot as he draws fists to sides.

114

300

301

302

303

303. Right partner remains stationary for movements 303, 304, 305. Left man takes step forward as he punches into midsection with right fist, slapping right upper arm with left hand as punch is made.

304. Without foot movement, left man continues with elbow blow to head, slapping right forearm with left hand.

305. Left man takes step back with right foot as he blocks downward with left forearm. (This is a simulated block against a second, imaginary opponent).

304   305

306

307

308

309

306. Left man steps forward with right foot to assume ready stance, as right man resumes fighting stance. (Same as stance in 301.)

307. Both men assume starting stance.

308. Both men resume starting stance. (Note that the next series will repeat the actions above, except from a different stance.)

309. Both men take step back with right foot to assume fighting stance.

310. Right man simulates attack by taking step forward with right foot and punching straight out with right fist, drawing left fist to side, while left man steps to the side with left foot and draws both fists to sides.

310   **311**

11. Right man remains motionless for movements 311, 312, 313. Left man punches straight into midsection with right fist as he takes step forward with right foot. He slaps right upper arm with left hand as the punch is made.

12. Without foot movement, he continues with the right elbow blow into the head, slapping right forearm with left hand.

312

13. He steps back with right foot as he blocks downward with left arm.

14. Both men resume fighting stance as in 309.

Both men resume starting stance. End of routine.

(There is no bow here. The bow is made only at the end of the full set of routines.)

313   314

asterisk indicates an action without a photo.

315   **316**   **317**

Second routine
* Starting position

315. Left man assumes palm-over-fist ready stance as right man steps back with right foot into fighting stance.

316. Right man steps forward with right foot and punches straight out with right fist. Left man sidesteps with left foot and blocks downward with left arm.

317. Left man steps to 45 degrees front and delivers high knuckle blow, palm down.

318. Left man steps back with right foot and blocks down with left arm.

* Return to positions in 315.

* Return to starting position.

319. Right man steps back with right foot into a low fist on-guard. Left man steps back with right foot and assumes overhead fist on-guard.

320. (The next moves are a repetition of the first section of the routine.) Right man delivers punch with right fist. Left man blocks.

318   **319**   **320**

321 **322**

321. Left man delivers high knuckle blow.

322. Left man blocks down with left arm.

* Return to stances, as in 319.

* Return to starting position. (End.)

323

Third routine

* Starting position.

323. Left man assumes palm-over-fist ready stance as right man steps back with right foot into fighting stance.

324. Right man punches with right fist; left man sidesteps, blocks downward with left arm.

325. Left man steps forward with right foot as he slashes with right open hand (palm up), left fist at side.

324 **325**

326 **327**

328 **329**

326. Left man draws right open-hand cross body and delivers palm down open-hand slash into neck.

327. Without foot movement, left man delivers kidney punch with left fist, drawing right fist to side.

328. Left man steps back with right foot and blocks down with left arm.

* Return to stances as in 323.

* Return to starting position.

329. Right man steps back into low fist on-guard as left man steps back into high slashing on-guard.

* Right man punches with right fist; left man sidesteps and blocks downward with left arm as in 324.

* Left man steps forward with right foot as he slashes with right open hand (palm up) as in 325.

* Left man draws right open-hand cross body and delivers palm-down open-hand slash into neck as in 326.

* Left man delivers kidney punch with left fist as in 327.

* Left man steps back with right foot and blocks down with left arm as in 328.

* Return to fighting stance as in 329.

* Return to starting position. (End.)

Fourth routine.

330

* Starting position.

* Left man takes step to left (with left foot) and assumes a palm-over-fist ready stance. Right man steps back with right foot as he assumes a low fist on-guard, right fist at his side.

* Right man steps forward with right foot as he punches straight out with right fist. Left man sidesteps with left foot as he blocks down with left arm.

330. Left man steps forward (at 45 degrees) with right foot as he delivers heel-of-the-palm blow upward toward the temple.

331. Left man steps back with right foot as he blocks down with left arm.

* Left man assumes palm-over-fist ready stance as right man assumes low fist on-guard.

* Return to starting position.

332. Left man takes step back with right foot as he assumes high, heel-of-palm fighting stance. Right man steps back with right foot into low fist on-guard.

* Right man steps forward, punching with right fist; left man side-steps, blocks down with left arm.

331   **332**

* Left man steps forward (45 degrees) with right foot as he delivers heel-of-the palm blow high, as in 330.

* Left man steps back with right foot as he blocks down with left arm, as in 331.

* Left man assumes high heel-of-palm stance; right man steps back into low fist on-guard as in 332.

* Return to starting position. (End.)

Fifth routine

333

* Starting position.

* Left man takes step to left with left foot, assuming palm-over-fist ready stance. Right man steps back with right foot as he assumes low, fist on-guard.

* Right man steps forward with right foot as he punches straight out with right fist. Left man sidesteps (45 degrees) with his left foot as he blocks down with left arm.

333. Left man steps forward (45 degrees) with right foot as he delivers hammer blow down with right fist, aiming at collar bone.

334. Left man delivers kidney punch with left fist.

* Left man steps back with right foot, blocking down with left arm.

* Left man assumes palm-over-fist ready stance and right man assumes low fist on-guard.

* Return to starting position.

335. Left man steps back with right foot, assuming overhead hammer blow fighting stance. Right man steps back into low fist on-guard.

334   **335**

*   Right man steps forward with right foot as he punches straight out with right fist. Left man sidesteps (45 degrees) with left foot as he blocks down with left arm.

*   Left man steps forward (45 degrees) with right foot as he delivers hammer blow down with right fist, aiming at collar bone, as in 333.

*   Left man delivers kidney punch with left fist, as in 334.

*   Left man steps back with right foot, blocking down with left arm.

*   Left man assumes overhead hammer blow fighting stance. Right man steps back into low fist on-guard.

*   Return to starting position. (End.)

Sixth routine

*   Starting position.

*   Left man takes step to left with left foot, assuming palm-over-fist ready stance. Right man steps back with right foot, assuming low fist on-guard.

*   Right man steps forward with right foot as he punches straight out with right fist. Left man sidesteps (45 degrees) with left foot as he blocks down with left arm.

336

337

336.   Left man steps forward (45 degrees) with his right foot as he delivers "Y" of the hand blow with right hand, aiming at throat.

337.   Left man delivers kidney punch with left fist.

*   Left man steps back with right foot, blocking down with left arm.

* Left man assumes palm-over-fist ready stance; right man assumes low fist on-guard.

* Return to starting position.

338

339

338. Left man steps back with right foot, assuming high "Y" of the hand fighting stance; right man steps back into low fist on-guard.

* Right man steps forward with right foot as he punches straight out with right fist. Left man sidesteps (45 degrees) with left foot as he blocks down with left arm.

* Left man steps forward (45 degrees) with right foot as he delivers "Y" of the hand blow with right hand, aiming at throat, as in 336.

* Left man delivers kidney punch with left fist, as in 337.

* Left man steps back with right foot, blocking down with left arm.

* Left man assumes high "Y" of the hand fighting stance; right man steps back into low fist on-guard, as in 338.

* Return to starting position.

339. Bow.

* Return to starting position. (End.)

Note: Bowing occurs only at the beginning of the first routine and c the completion of the sixth routine.

INTRODUCTION TO THE FORMS

Like the Routines, the Forms are stylized arrangements of Karate blows, kicks, blocks, and leaps used against an imaginary adversary. Forms are meant as training practice similar to scales in piano practice. Learning scales alone does not give a student the ability to play Chopin, neither does learning Forms alone give the student street defense or contest ability; but it is one of the ways in which the basics of the art can be practiced. For exercise and body discipline, the Forms are excellent. They aid in developing co-ordination and agility

The student who is interested exclusively in Karate self-defense need not learn the Forms, though they are splendid for extra practice.

HOW TO PRACTICE FORMS

Practice of the Forms is done in a dramatic, exaggerated style. The punches, blocks, and kicks are executed with snap, vigor, and driving action. The slow movements are executed in a deliberate, intense manner. Each blow should be accompanied by a super-power shout or silent breath control. When demonstrated for belt degree ratings, the Forms must show technical excellence.

In the text for Forms and Routines: *Front* always refers to the position you were facing when you started. *Forward* always means stepping in the direction you are facing *at the moment*. For instance, you may be instructed to take a step *forward* to the *front* (which means that you are then facing *front*) or you may be asked to take a step *forward* to the rear (which means that you should be facing rear when you are told to take the step). *Rear* always means the direction behind your starting position, and *backward* always means the direction which is behind you at the moment. For instance, you may be told to take a step backward to the front (which means you would then be facing rear), or you could be told to take a step backward to the rear (which means you would at that moment be facing front). To help you follow the text, imagine that you are side-by-side with the man in the photo. When you start, you are both facing the same direction. When his back is turned (in the photo), so also should your back be turned to your original starting point. Do not be discouraged if you lose your way when you first start to do the Forms and Routines. All beginners make mistakes and so will you. It is only with patience and practice that you will make progress.

PURPLE BELT FORMS

First form

340. All one-man formal exercises begin with the position shown. Stand erect, feet slightly apart, fists held at thighs.

341. Bow from waist.

* Return to the position in 340.

342. Without moving right foot, step to side with left foot, block outward with left forearm, draw right fist to side.

343. Without moving left foot, kick with right foot as you punch with right fist straight out, drawing right fist to side.

340   **341**   **342**   **343**

344. Place right foot down to face front (do not take step with left foot; just pivot on the ball of the foot to get into front position), as you draw both fists to sides.

345. Without moving left foot, step to side with right foot as you block outward with right forearm and draw left fist to side.

346. Without moving right foot, kick with left foot as you punch out with left fist and draw right fist to side.

344   **345**   **346**   **347**

348 **349** **350** **351**

352 **353** **354** **355**

347. Place left foot down to face front (pivoting on ball of right foot) as you draw both fists to sides.

348. Step forward with left foot as you block up with left forearm.

349. Step forward with right foot as you block up with right forearm and draw left fist to side.

350. Step forward with left foot as you block up with left forearm and draw right fist to side.

351. Keeping right foot in place, step to side with left foot, blocking downward with left arm.

352. Step out with right foot, punching with right fist and drawing left fist to side.

353. Pivoting on the ball of left foot, turn 180 degrees clockwise, blocking downward with right arm and drawing left fist to side.

354. Step out with left foot as you punch with left fist, drawing right fist to side.

55. Pivoting on the ball of left foot, step to the rear with right foot you block down with right forearm and draw left fist to side.

356. Take another step to rear with left foot, blocking down with left arm, drawing right fist to side.

357. Take another step to rear with right foot as you block down with right arm and draw left fist to side.

358. Pivot on ball of right foot, clockwise, make 90 degree turn to face side, placing left foot forward. As you turn, draw open right hand, palm up, to side and assume slashing on-guard position with left hand.

359. Without moving left foot, step at 45 degrees with right foot as you draw left open hand, palm up, to side and slash with right open hand.

360. Pivot on ball of left foot, turn clockwise to face right side. As you turn, right hand assumes slashing on-guard position.

361. Without moving right foot, step to 45 degrees with left foot, clockwise, drawing right open hand to your side as left hand slashes.

362. Step back with left foot so that you face front. As you step, draw fists to sides.

363. Take small step with left foot to bring feet into starting position; place fists at thighs. Bow.

364. Resume starting position. (End.)

356   357   358   359

360 **361** **362**

Second form

363 **364**

365. Starting position.

366. Bow.

* Return to starting position.

367. Without moving right foot, step to left side with left foot as you block outward with left forearm.

368. Keep left foot in place. Punch out with right fist as you kick with right foot.

365 **366** **367** **368**

369. Place right foot down to face front as you draw both fists to sides.

370. Keep feet in place as you turn body at 45 degrees to the right, blocking upward with left forearm and punching forward with right fist.

371. Take step back with right foot and assume slashing on-guard, right hand raised.

372. Take a step back with your left foot and assume slashing on-guard, left hand raised.

369   370   371   372

373. Step forward with left foot as you punch forward with left fist, drawing right fist to side.

374. Step forward with right foot, making backhanded right slash as left palm slaps right upper arm.

375. Without stepping, pivot on balls of both feet, making counter-clockwise turn to face rear. As you turn, block upward with left forearm and stab upward with right hand, palm up.

376. No foot movement. Assume slashing on-guard, right hand raised.

373   374   375   376

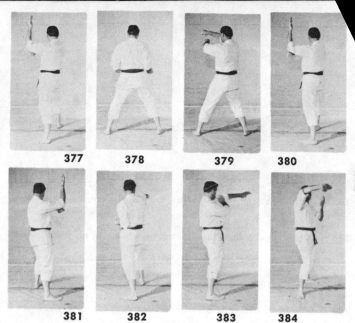

377. Take step back with left foot and change to slashing on-guard with left hand raised.

378. Step forward with left foot (still facing rear) and draw both fists to sides.

379. (Note that we are now repeating the movements from 370, but facing rear.) Without foot movement, turn body ¼ turn to left, blocking upward with right forearm and punching forward with left fist.

380. Step back with left foot and assume slashing on-guard, left hand raised.

381. Step back with right foot, changing to slashing on-guard, with right hand raised.

382. Step forward (to rear) with right foot as you punch with right fist.

383. Step with left foot as you slash outward with left open hand. As you slash, right palm slaps left upper arm.

384. Without stepping, pivot on balls of both feet, making 180 degree turn, clockwise, to face front. As you turn, slash upward with right forearm and poke upward with left hand, palm up.

385   **386**   **387**   **388**

385. Without foot movement, place arms in slashing on-guard, left hand raised.

386. Step back with right foot, shift arms to slashing on-guard, right hand raised.

387. Step forward with right foot, facing front, as you draw both fists to sides.

388. Take small step with left foot to bring feet to starting position.

*   Bow.

*   Return to starting position. (End.)

     Third form

*   Assume starting position.

*   Bow.

*   Return to starting position.

389. Keep right foot in place, step to side with left foot as you block outward with left forearm.

     389   **390**   **391**

390. Keep left foot in place as you kick with right foot, punch with right fist, and draw left fist to side.

391. Place right foot down to face front, drawing fists to sides.

392. Take step back with left foot as you block outward with right forearm, drawing left fist to side.

393. Take step back with right foot, blocking downward with left forearm, drawing right fist to side.

394. Take step back with left foot, making backhanded knuckle blow with right fist.

395. Pivot on ball of right foot, step clockwise with left foot so that you face right side. As you step, make double block upward with forearms crossed.

396. No foot movement. Draw fists to sides.

397. Pivot on ball of left foot, step counterclockwise with right foot to make 180 degree turn, facing left side. As you turn, make crossed-arm block upward.

398. No foot movement. Draw fists to sides.

399. Without stepping, pivot on balls of both feet to turn facing front. As you turn, place fists palm-over-palm (closed) at left side.

400. Step forward with left foot as you punch out with left fist.

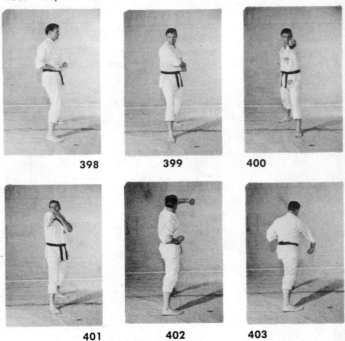

398   399   400

401   402   403

401. Step forward with right foot as you make right elbow blow forward, striking right forearm with left palm.

402. Without stepping, pivot on balls of both feet, turning counter-clockwise to face rear, blocking upward with left forearm and drawing right fist to side.

403. Keeping right foot in place, take short step forward (to rear) with left foot as you block down with right forearm, drawing left fist to side.

404. No foot movement. Make backhanded knuckle blow with right fist.

405. Turning clockwise, pivot on the ball of the right foot, step around with left foot so that you face front, arms in crossed block upward.

406. No foot movement. Draw fists to sides.

* Return to starting position.

* Bow.

* Return to starting position. (End.)

404

405

406

Fourth form

* Assume starting position.

* Bow.

* Return to starting position.

407. Keep right foot in place, take step to left side with left foot as you block outward with left forearm, drawing right fist to side.

408. Keep left foot in place as you kick with right foot, punch with right fist and draw left fist to side.

407

408

409 **410** **411**

409. Place right foot down so that you face front, drawing both fists to sides.

410. Sidestep with left foot as you punch straight down with both fists.

411. No foot movement. Moving arms in broad, outward gesture, cross forearms at chest.

412 **413** **414** **415**

412. Block sharply upward with both forearms.

413. Return arms to crossed position at chest.

414. Step back with left foot so that you face left side. Punch downward with right fist, drawing left fist to side.

415. Step back with right foot so that you face front. Block upward with left forearm, drawing left fist to side.

416. Keeping right foot in position, place left foot at right knee and bring fists, palm-over-palm, to right side.

417. Kick with left foot, block up with left forearm, and stab forward with right hand—all three actions simultaneous.

418. Recover by placing left foot down (crossed over right foot), and bringing hands back.

| 416 | 417 | 418 |

419. Take step back with right foot, bringing both fists, palm-over-palm (closed) to right side. (Note: The action in this form is from positions 417 to 419. Position 418 is actually a transition between the two and is shown to help you follow the instruction. There is no hesitation at position 418.)

420. Keeping left foot in position, kick forward with right foot as you make hammer blow with right fist and draw left fist to side.

421. As you place right foot down, make forward blow with left forearm and draw right fist to side.

422. Keep right foot in position as you step to side with left foot and stab forward with right hand.

| 419 | 420 | 421 | 422 |

423 **424** **425** **426**

423. Step forward with right foot as you make elbow blow forward with right elbow, slapping right forearm with left hand.

424. Step forward with left foot as you punch forward with left fist, drawing right fist to side.

425. Step forward with right foot as you punch forward with right fist, drawing left fist to side.

426. Step back with right foot so that you are in the ready stance.

* Return to starting position.

* Bow.

* Return to starting position. (End.)

REQUIREMENTS FOR SPORT KARATE BELT DEGREES

WHITE BELT (6th Degree). Beginner. As soon as a student begins his training in Karate, he is designated White Belt.

WHITE BELT (5th Degree). The Karate instructor, at his discretion, designates the student as 5th degree White Belt on the basis of his work and attitude. There is no formal test for 5th Degree White Belt, but the student is expected to know pertinent facts relating to Karate safety procedures (including control of blows), twenty hand blows, twenty foot blows and basic blocking techniques, and have some knowledge of striking areas.

PURPLE BELT (4th Degree). Six two-man routines, well executed. Five one-man forms, well executed. Working knowledge of one-point free-style practice.

BROWN BELT (3rd Degree). Six additional routines, executed to perfection. Competition in free-style, winning at least two matche against two different Purple Belt opponents.

BROWN BELT (2nd Degree). Twelve additional routines, executed to perfection. Five Karate trips and throws. Competition in free-style, winning at least two matches against two different 3rd Degree Brown Belt opponents.

BROWN BELT (1st Degree). One 90-movement form. Competition in free-style, winning at least two matches against two different 2nd Degree Brown Belt opponents.

FIRST DEGREE BLACK BELT. Five one-man slow forms, executed to perfection. Competition in free-style. Winning at least two matches against two different 1st Degree Brown Belt opponents.

All Degrees require that the student exhibit general qualities of good character and sportsmanship.

427

Fifth form

* Assume starting position.

* Bow.

* Return to starting position.

427. Take step to side with left foot, blocking outward with left forearm and drawing right fist to hip.

428. Kick with right foot as you punch out with right fist, drawing left fist to side.

429. Place right foot down so that you face front in ready stance.

430. Sidestep with left foot as you punch straight down with both fists.

428   **429**   **430**

431. No foot movement. Moving arms in broad, outward gesture, cross forearms at chest.

432. Block sharply upward with both forearms.

433. Return arms to crossed position at chest.

434. No foot movement. Deliver side hammer blow to right with right fist, placing left open hand (palm down) under right forearm.

435. No foot movement. Make backhanded knuckle blow with right fist as you draw left fist to side.

436. No foot movement. Block downward with left forearm as you draw right fist to side.

437. (Face left front for 437, 438, and 439.) Deliver hammer blow downward with right fist as you kick forward with right foot, drawing left fist to side. The action in this movement is cross-body.

438. Place right foot down, then make forward thrust with left forearm as you draw right fist to side.

431   432   433   434

435   436   437   438

439 **440** **441** **442**

439. No foot movement. Make forward thrust with right forearm, as you draw left fist to side.

440. Without stepping, pivot on balls of both feet, turning counter-clockwise to face rear; placing closed fists palm over palm at right side.

441. (This is intermediate to 440 and 442, there is no hesitation at 441.) Take step to rear with right foot.

442. Take a step to rear with left foot and then pivot on balls of both feet, turning body clockwise to face front. As you turn, place fists at left side.

443. Pivot on the ball of right foot, stepping around clockwise with left foot so that you face right side. As you turn, punch out with left fist, drawing right fist to right side.

444. Step forward (to right side) with right foot as you strike with left elbow, slapping left forearm with right hand.

445. Without stepping, pivot on balls of both feet, turning counter-clockwise to face left side. Then, place left foot at right knee as you block downward with left forearm and draw right fist to side.

443 **444** **445**

446. Place left foot on the ground as you block upward with left forearm, right fist to side.

447. Punch downward with right fist.

446 447 448 449

448. Recover to position in 446.

449. (This is a transition between 448 and 450. There is no hesitation at 449.) Take step forward with right foot. Then, moving counterclockwise, pivot on balls of both feet and turn 180 degrees to face right side.

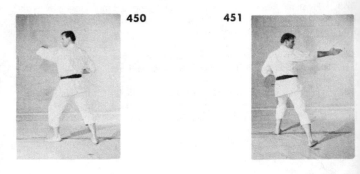

450 451

450. As you complete turn, make blow straight out with left forearm as you draw right fist to side.

451. Take step to rear with left foot as you stab to left side with right open hand.

452. Take step to left side with right foot as you make elbow blow with right elbow and slap right forearm with left hand.

* Moving counterclockwise, take step around with right foot so that you face front again.

453. Assume ready stance.

* Assume starting position.

* Bow.

* Assume starting position. (End.)

452

453

DIGEST OF RULES REGULATING KARATE CONTEST

Contestants wear the regulation uniform (Karate Gi) and are required to have fingernails and toenails short and smooth. Body is to be clean. Contestants with conditioned striking points must pad and bandage them for contest.

Contest area is not less than 20' x 20' and may range up to 40' x 40'. Area is square and has a smooth-surface floor.

Judges are normally three or five in number: one referee judge who moves about; others are placed at opposite sides of contest area. Other officials (timekeeper, scorekeeper, etc.) are seated off the contest area in full view of proceedings.

Time of matches is ordinarily two minutes for lower rank contestants and three to five minutes for higher ranks. Referee judge may rule extension of appointed time.

American students will understand how points are made in Karate contest if they will keep in mind that like fencing (and unlike boxing), you must *theoretically* endanger your opponent *without actually making contact*. In other words, if your opponent fails to block or otherwise avoid your blow, and you can be seen to have the opportunity to deliver it, you score.

Match may be stopped if actual contact is made with opponent,

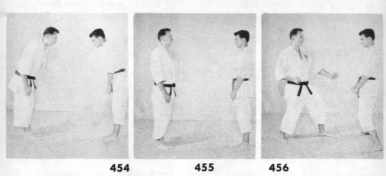

454   **455**   **456**

whether or not injury results. Match may be stopped for unnecessary body contact (shoving, bumping, etc.), ignoring instructions of referee judge, stalling, finger stab blows directed too close to opponent's eyes, loss of temper, throwing techniques not allowed in Karate, or other unsportsmanlike conduct. (Throwing and tripping techniques are reserved for higher degree matches.)

Points are given for properly directed and executed blows stopped approximately two inches from the target area. It is determined beforehand whether matches are to be won for single point or for two-out-of-three points. It is determined beforehand whether decision matches are allowed. Decision matches are scored on the basis of tactics, style, and fighting spirit.

THIRD BROWN BELT ROUTINES

First two-man routine

454.   Bow. (You will not bow again until all six forms have been completed.)

455.   Position of attention.

456.   Left man steps back with right foot and assumes fist on-guard stance. Right man steps to the side with left foot and assumes ready stance, fists at thighs. Both men move simultaneously throughout.

457.   Left man steps forward with right foot and attacks with downward, right hand punch as he draws left fist to left hip. Right man steps forward with left foot and blocks downward with left forearm as he draws right fist to right hip.

144

| **457** | **458** | **459** |

458. With foot movement, right man punches with right fist into the upper body as he draws left fist to left hip. Left man remains in position.

459. Left man steps back with right foot and assumes left on-guard stance. Right man steps back with left foot and assumes ready stance.

Both men return to the position of attention as in 455. (End.)
The form should be repeated by reversing attack to the right side; then, it should be practiced by reversing the positions of the two men.

Second two-man routine

460. Position of attention.

461. Left man steps back with right foot and assumes left fist on-guard stance. Right man sidesteps with left foot and assumes ready stance.

| **460** | **461** |

462

463

462. Left man steps forward with right foot and punches straight out with right fist as he draws left fist to hip. Right man steps back with right foot as he blocks with inside edge of left forearm (palm toward his face) as he draws right fist to right hip.

463. Left man stays in position. Right man counters with straight right punch into middle body and draws left fist to hip. There is no foot movement.

* Return to the position in 461.
* Return to the position in 460. (End.)

The Form should then be practiced by first reversing the side of attack, then the positions of the men. This procedure should be followed in all subsequent Form practice.

464

465

Third two-man routine

464. Position of attention.

465. Left man steps back with right foot and assumes left on-guard stance. Right man sidesteps with left foot and assumes ready stance

466. Left man steps forward with right foot and punches toward head with right fist as he draws left fist back to hip. Right man steps back with right foot and slashes up and out with left hand as he draws right hand to hip.

467. Left man stays in position. Right man counters with stabbing blow into middle body (palm in) as he draws left open hand to hip (palm up).

* Both men return to the position in 465.

* Position of attention. (End.)

466 **467**

Fourth two-man routine

468. Position of attention.

469. Left man steps back with right foot and assumes fist on-guard stance. Right man sidesteps with left foot and assumes ready stance.

470. Left man steps forward with right foot and punches high with right fist as he draws left fist to hip. Right man steps back with right foot as he blocks up and out with left forearm and draws right hand to hip. The slashing hand is kept open, fingers curled.

468   **469**   **470**

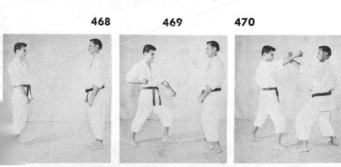

471. Left man stays in position. Right man grabs cloth at elbow with left hand and pulls forward as he punches into face with right fist.

472. Left man steps back with right foot into fist on-guard as right man steps into ready stance.

* Return to position of attention. (End.)

Fifth two-man routine

473. Position of attention.

474. Left man steps back with right foot into fist on-guard stance. Right man sidesteps with left foot into ready stance.

475. Left man steps forward with right foot and punches high with right fist as he draws left fist to hip. Left man steps back with right foot and blocks up with forearm horizontal as he draws right fist to hip.

476. Left man stays in position. Right man punches into middle body with right fist as he draws left fist to hip.

477. Left man steps back with right foot and assumes fist on-guard position as right man steps back with left foot and assumes ready stance.

Return to position of attention. (End.)

476

477

Sixth two-man routine

478. Position of attention.

479. Left man steps back with right foot into fist on-guard stance as right man sidesteps with left foot into ready stance.

478

479

480

480. Left man steps forward with right foot and punches straight out with right fist as he draws left fist to hip. Right man steps back with right foot and parries blow with outside edge of left forearm and draws right fist to hip.

481

482

483

484

481. Left man stays in position. Right man counters with punch into middle body with right fist as he draws left fist to hip.

482. Left man steps back with right foot into fist on-guard stance as right man steps back with left foot into ready stance.

483. Position of attention. (End.)

484. Bow. This bow indicates the completion of all six forms of this series.

THIRD BROWN BELT FORMS
First form

485. Position of attention.

486. Bow.

487. Position of attention.

485   486   487   488   489

488. Step to left with left foot; block down with left arm (as though blocking low punch or kick). Bring right fist to hip, palm up. Both fist movements are made as you step into position.

489. Step to left with right foot as you punch straight out with right fist. Bring left fist to left hip as right fist punches.

490   491   492   493

490. Pivot on ball of left foot, step to right with right foot, turning clockwise 180 degrees as you block down with right fist, drawing left fist to hip (palm up).

491. Step to right with left foot as you punch straight out with left fist, drawing right fist to hip.

492. Pivot on the ball of right foot, step to front with left foot. Keep right fist at hip and, as you step, block down with left fist.

493. Step to front with right foot as you block up with right forearm and draw left fist to hip.

494. Step to front with left foot as you block up with left forearm and draw right fist to hip.

495. Step to front with right foot, as you block up with right forearm, drawing left fist to hip.

496. Step to right with right foot and block down with right fist, as you draw left fist to hip.

497. Step to right with left foot as you punch straight out with left fist, drawing right fist to hip.

494   495   496   497

498. Step to left with right foot (clockwise) as you block down with right fist and draw left fist to hip.

499. Step to left with left foot as you punch straight out with left fist, drawing right fist to hip.

500. Step to the rear with left foot (counterclockwise) as you block down with left fist, drawing right fist to hip.

501. Step to rear with right foot, punching straight out with right fist, drawing left fist to hip.

498   499   500   501

502   **503**   **504**   **505**

502. Step to rear with left foot, punching straight out with left fist, drawing right fist to hip.

503. Step to rear with right foot as you punch straight out with right fist, drawing left fist to hip.

504. Pivot on the ball of right foot (clockwise) and step into "T" position to left with left foot. As you step, bring left hand into slashing open-hand extended vertical position while right hand is brought into horizontal, open-hand (palm-up) position at hip.

505. Step to left front (at 45 degree angle) with right foot as you slash to left front with right open hand, drawing left hand to hip in palm-up open-hand position.

506. Pivot on ball of left foot and step to right with right foot (clockwise) assuming "T" position with right foot forward. Right hand is moved into an extended slashing on-guard while you bring left hand to hip in palm-up, open-hand position.

507. With left foot step to right front (at a 45 degree angle) as you slash to the right front with left hand open and draw right hand to hip.

506   **507**

508 **509** **510**

508. Step back with left foot to face front and draw both fists to hips, palm up. Feet are apart, knees slightly bent.

509. Bring feet together and place fists (palm in) at thighs.

510. Bow.

* Return to position of attention. (End.)

511 **512** **513** **514** **515**

Second form

511. Position of attention.

512. Bow.

513. Return to position of attention.

514. Sidestep with left foot to place feet shoulder-width apart. As you sidestep, in a rounded motion slowly bring fists to sides, palm up. (This is the ready stance which will be used in much of the Form training.)

515. Slowly raise right fist to horizontal position at head as you raise left fist to shoulder level at left side. As you make arm movements, pivot on ball of left foot, point toe, and turn body to left.

516 **517** **518** **519**

516. Without moving feet, drop right fist down and make quick uppercut blow as you place left fist at right shoulder.

517. Take short step to left with left foot as you draw right fist to right hip and strike a sharp hammer blow to the side.

518. Keep left foot in position, turn body to right as you draw right foot back in "T" position As you move your body, slowly bring left fist above head and place right fist out.

519. Without foot movement, bring right fist to left shoulder as you drop left arm and make snappy uppercut blow.

520. Take short step to right side with right foot and as you draw left fist to left hip, strike sharp side hammer blow with right hand.

521. Keep left foot in position and bring right foot to left knee as you place right fist over left fist.

522. Make simultaneous right hand and right foot blow at a 45 degree angle to rear. The hand makes a side hammer blow and the kick is a side-snap.

520 **521** **522**

523 **524** **525** **526** **527**

523. Place right foot down under you. Step forward with left foot as you deliver sharp slash straight out with left hand and bring right hand to hip.

524. Take step forward with right foot as you slash forward with right hand and bring left hand to hip.

525. Take step forward with left foot and slash forward with left hand as you place right hand at hip.

526. Take step forward with right foot as you stab forward with right hand and place left hand palm down at right armpit.

527, 528. Without lifting right foot, pivot on it and turn body clockwise to face right. As you turn, place right hand at hip and place left hand in on-guard slashing position.

528 **529** **530**

529. From position in 528, step forward at 45 degree angle with right foot as you slash forward with right hand and bring left hand to hip, palm up.

530. Turn body clockwise 135 degrees without lifting left foot, pivot it as you keep hands in same position as in 529.

531. From position in 530, step forward at 45 degree angle with left foot as you slash with left hand and draw right hand to hip, palm up.

532. Keep your right foot in position, take step (45 degrees counter-clockwise) with left foot as you swing both arms back and up, right palm down and left palm up. Shift weight to left foot.

533. Without foot movement, bring right fist down and around and make back knuckle blow as you bring left fist to your hip.

534. With right foot, stamp kick high at 45 degree angle to right. Left foot stays in position. There is no arm movement.

531 532 533 534

535. Place right foot down on floor as you punch straight out with left fist and draw right fist to hip, palm up.

536. Take short step to rear with right foot and turn body counter-clockwise 45 degrees as you swing arms up and back, left palm down, right palm up.

537. Without foot movement, swing left fist down and around and make a back knuckle blow as you place right fist at hip.

535   536   537

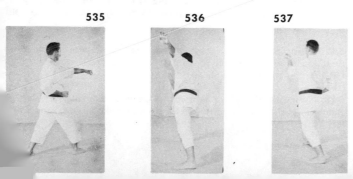

538. Keep right foot in position, kick high with left foot. There is no arm movement.

539. Place left foot down and punch with right fist straight out, keeping left fist at hip.

540. From the position in 539, take step forward with right foot and assume right on-guard stance with right fist extended and left fist still at hip.

538   539   540

541   542   543

541. Pivot on ball of left foot, step with right foot 135 degrees clockwise, and block down vigorously with right forearm. Left fist remains at hip.

542. Pivot on ball of right foot, turn body clockwise 45 degrees, and step around with left foot in front. As you turn, block up with left forearm and place right fist at hip.

543. Without lifting left foot, pivot on it and take short step to right with right foot as you block down with right forearm and bring left fist to hip.

544 **545** **546** **547**

544. From the position in 543, take step forward with left foot as you block up with left forearm and bring right fist to hip.

545. Return to the ready stance. (You should now face the same direction as when you started the form.)

546. Position of attention.

547. Bow. (End.)

Third form

* Position of attention.

* Bow.

* Position of attention.

548. Without moving right foot, step to left side with left foot as you block out with left forearm and draw right fist to hip.

549. Without moving left foot, draw right foot up to it. There is no arm movement.

548 **549**

550. Without foot movement, snap left fist down as you snap right fist up to face height. The fist movements are simultaneous, and the downward fist moves on the inside.

551. Without foot movement, reverse fists so that left fist is at face height and right fist is down. The downward fist moves inside.

552. Pivot on the ball of left foot and place right foot to rear (move clockwise 180 degrees) as you block up and out with right forearm and place left fist at hip.

553. Keep your right foot in position and slide left foot beside it. There is no arm movement.

| 550 | 551 | 552 | 553 |

554. Without foot movement, block down with right fist as you block up with left fist.

555. Without foot movement, reverse the position, blocking down with left fist and up with right fist. (The downward fist moves inside.)

556. Take step with left foot (to face starting position) and block out with left arm as you bring right fist to hip.

557. Keeping left foot in position, take step forward with right foot as you stab forward with right hand, bringing left fist to hip.

| 554 | 555 | 556 | 557 |

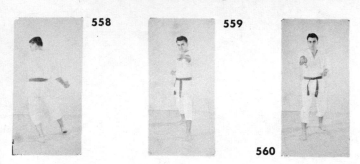

558, 559. Making a full turn, pivot on the ball of left foot and step around (counterclockwise) with right foot so that you assume a "T" position with left foot forward. As you turn, right fist is brought to hip and left arm swings around to execute outward hammer blow as you complete the turn.

560. Keeping left foot in position, step forward with right foot as you punch straight out with right fist, bringing left fist to hip.

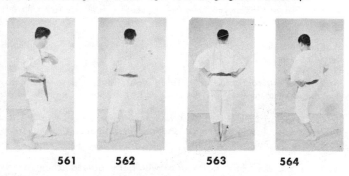

561, 562. Without lifting feet, pivot on balls of both feet turning counterclockwise to face rear. As you pivot, arms are placed in the position shown in 561. When you face rear, execute a straight punch with right fist as you draw left fist to hip, and step to rear with right foot. 561 and 562 constitute a continuous motion. There is no hesitation between them.

563. (You should now be facing to the rear of your starting position.) Bring left foot up to right foot and place fists at hips.

564. Keep left foot in position, turn upper body to left (45 degrees), and kick straight out from that position. There is no arm movement.

565. Place right foot down and twist body only (counterclockwise). As you twist, make elbow blow with right arm without moving fists.

566. Without foot movement, swing right fist around and deliver back knuckle blow as you bring left fist to hip.

567. Pivot on ball of right foot and turn 90 degrees (clockwise), placing fists at hips as you turn, and execute a forward kick with left foot.

568. Place left foot down and twist body clockwise, striking with left elbow as you twist.

569. Without foot movement, bring right fist to hip as you make circular movement with left fist and deliver backhand knuckle blow.

570. Pivot on ball of left foot and turn (counterclockwise) 90 degrees as you place fists at hips and deliver stamping kick with right foot at the completion of turn.

571. Place right foot down and twist body around (counterclockwise) as you strike elbow blow with right elbow, keeping fists at hips.

572. Without foot movement, make circular motion with right fist and deliver backhand knuckle blow as you place left fist at hip.

573. Moving clockwise, step to rear with left foot (pivot on ball of right foot; do not lift it from the floor) and punch straight out with left fist as you bring right fist to hip.

574. Leave left foot in position; take step with right foot so that feet are parallel. As you step, bring left fist to hip and place right fist at left shoulder.

575. Moving clockwise, pivot on ball of right foot, stepping around with left foot to face starting position. There is no arm movement.

573 574 575 576

577 578 579 580

576, 577. Leap to right side and as you execute leap, reverse position of fists so that right fist is at hip and left fist is at right shoulder when you complete the leap.

578. Ready stance.

579. Position of attention.

580. Bow. (End.)

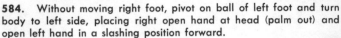

Fourth form

* Position of attention.

581. Bow.

582. Position of attention.

583. Ready stance.

584. Without moving right foot, pivot on ball of left foot and turn body to left side, placing right open hand at head (palm out) and open left hand in a slashing position forward.

585. Pivot on balls of feet, without lifting them, turn (clockwise) to right side, and reverse position of open hands so that right hand is in slashing position forward and left hand is at head.

586. Keep right foot in position, step forward with left foot, and block down with crossed arms.

587. Keep left foot in position, step forward with right foot as you block with right forearm, and place left fist at right elbow (palm down).

| 588 | 589 | 590 |

588. Keep right foot in position. Place fists palm over palm at right hip as you bring left foot to right knee.

589. With left hand, make back fist blow as you snap kick with left foot.

590. Place left foot down and hit with circular elbow blow with right elbow as left palm strikes right forearm.

| 591 | 592 | 593 |

591. Pivot on ball of left foot, without lifting it, so that body faces front and head is turned to right side. As you turn, place fists palm over palm at left hip and bring right foot to left knee.

592. Kick to right side, using snap kick, as you make backhand fist blow with right fist, leaving left fist at hip.

593. Place right foot down, keep left foot in position, and turn body (clockwise), striking with left elbow as right palm strikes left forearm.

594   595   596   597

594. No foot movement. Turn body counterclockwise to face front as you block up with left forearm and slash forward with right hand.

595. Keeping left foot in position, kick forward high with right foot as you bring fists palm over palm to left hip.

596. From position shown in 595, leap forward to land in the "T" position shown in 596 as you deliver backhand knuckle blow with right fist. Left fist remains at hip.

597, 598. Without lifting right foot from floor, pivot on ball of right foot, stepping around clockwise with your left foot 135 degrees. As you turn, bring left fist to on-guard position and place right fist at left elbow.

599. From position in 598, kick forward high with left foot. No arm movement.

600. As you place left foot down, punch straight out with left fist as you bring right fist to hip.

598   599   600

601 602 603

601. Keep right foot in position and step out with left foot, shifting weight to left foot. As you step, punch straight out with right fist and bring left fist to hip.

602. Keeping left foot in position, turn body (clockwise) and slide right foot so that you have turned 90 degrees from position in 601. As you turn, place right fist in on-guard position and place left fist at right elbow.

603. Without arm movement, kick high with right foot.

604. As you place right foot on floor, punch out with right fist as you bring left fist to hip.

605. Keep left foot in position, taking step out with right foot and shifting weight to right foot. As you step out, punch with left fist and bring right fist to hip.

606. Keep right foot in place, turn body (counterclockwise) 90 degrees from position in 605. Bring left foot forward as you turn. Block backhanded with left forearm and place right fist at left elbow.

604 605 606

607. Keep left foot in position, step (clockwise) with right foot to face 90 degrees from 606. As you step, block backhanded with right forearm and place left fist at right elbow.

608. Keep right foot in position, step (counterclockwise) with left foot so that body is 90 degrees from position in 607 As you step, block backhanded with left forearm and place right fist at left elbow.

609. Keep right foot in position and step to rear with left foot as you extend both arms upward.

607   608   609   610

610. As you swing both arms down and back, deliver high knee kick with right knee and raise body onto ball of left foot.

611. From knee kick, place right foot down and without interruption of motion, pivot counterclockwise on the balls of both feet to face front; when facing front (still without interrupted movement) take step forward with left foot as you slash with left hand and place right fist at hip.

612. Keep left foot in position, step forward with right foot as you slash with right hand, and bring left fist to hip.

613. Step with your right foot into the ready stance.

* Position of attention.

* Bow.

* Position of attention. (End.)

611 612 613

Fifth form

* Position of attention.

* Bow.

614. Position of attention.

615. Keep right foot in position, take step to left with left foot as you block out and back with left forearm, and place right fist at hip.

614 615 616 617

616. Without moving right foot, take another step with left foot as you punch straight out with right fist and place left fist at hip.

617. Slide right foot up to left foot as you turn to face forward. As you turn, place right arm in horizontal position, palm up and place left fist at right elbow, palm down.

618. Without moving left foot, take step to right with right foot as you block out and back with right forearm and place left fist at hip.

619. Without moving left foot, take another step with right foot as you punch straight out with left fist and bring right fist to hip.

620. Without moving right foot, slide left foot up to right foot as you turn to face forward. As you turn, place left arm in horizontal position palm up and place right fist at left elbow.

621. As you take step forward with right foot, strike outward with right forearm as you place left fist at right elbow.

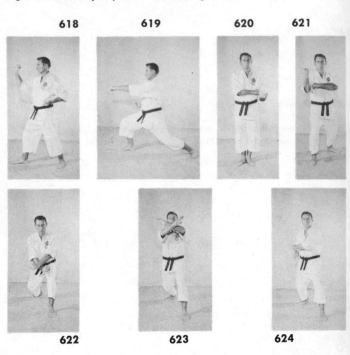

618   619   620   621

622   623   624

622. Take a step forward with left foot as you block down with crossed forearms.

623. No foot work. Block up with open hands, crossed forearms.

624. No foot work. Place right fist at hip, palm up as you place left fist over it palm down.

| 625 | 626 | 627 | 628 |

625, 626. One continuous motion. Without moving feet, swing arms to reverse the position in 624; then punch straight out with left fist as you bring right fist to hip.

627. Step forward with right foot as you punch straight out with right fist and bring left fist to hip.

628. Moving counterclockwise, pivot on ball of left foot and turn 180 degrees placing right foot forward at end of turn. As you turn, block down with right forearm. Left fist remains at hip.

| 629 | 630 | 631 |

629. Pivot on both feet, turning counterclockwise, to face front, slashing front with left hand. Right fist remains at hip.

630. Without moving left foot, kick left hand with bottom of right foot. Right fist is at hip.

631. From the position in 630, leap forward and land with right foot forward in "T" position. As you leap, strike right elbow blow, hitting left palm against right forearm.

632

633

634

632. Keeping right foot in position, slide left foot up to it placing most weight on forward foot and placing ball of left foot lightly on floor. As you slide foot, make backhand knuckle blow with right fist and place left fist at elbow, palm down.

633. Without lifting right foot, pivot on ball of right foot, turning counterclockwise 180 degrees to face rear, taking small step out with left foot. Keep arms in same position as for 632.

634, 635. Leap and turn counterclockwise 90 degrees. Land with feet crossed and knees bent, blocking down with crossed fists.

635

636

637

636. Keeping left foot in position, rise and step to rear with right foot, turn body to rear as you block sidewards with right forearm, and place left fist at right elbow.

637. Without lifting right foot, pivot on the ball of right foot, turning counterclockwise 180 degrees to face front. Place left foot well forward and put most of weight on left foot. As you turn and step, stab down with right open hand (palm up) and bring left open hand to right shoulder (palm up).

638. Without lifting feet, shift weight back onto right foot and assume fist on-guard position.

639. Take long step forward with right foot and place most of weight on right foot. As you step, stab down with left open hand (palm up) and place right open hand at left shoulder (palm up).

640. Without moving feet, shift weight back onto left foot and assume right fist on-guard position.

* Step back with your right foot into a ready stance.

* Bow.

* Position of attention. (Fnd.)

| 638 | 639 | 640 |

SECOND BROWN BELT TWO-MAN ROUTINES
First routine

641. Starting position.

642. Bow.

641 642

643 644

643. Both men step back with right foot into low fist on-guard.

644. Right man steps forward with right foot and punches low with right fist; left man slidesteps† forward and blocks down with left forearm.

645 646

645. Left man punches with right fist into midsection.

646. Left man punches with left fist into midsection.

647 648

647. Left man slidesteps back into low fist on-guard; right man steps back with right foot into low fist on-guard.

648. Return to starting position. (End.)

† Slidestep: Refer to introductory material in which slidestep is explained.

Second routine

* Starting position.

* Both men step back with right foot into low fist on-guard.

649. Right man steps forward with right foot and punches straight out with right fist; left man slide-steps forward and parries cross-body with left forearm.

649

650   651

650. Left man punches with right fist into midsection.

651. Aiming at head, left man delivers left elbow blow.

* Left man slidesteps back into low fist on-guard, right man steps back with right foot into low fist on-guard.

* Return to starting position. (End.)

Third routine

* Starting position.

* Both men step back with right foot into low fist on-guard.

652. Right man steps forward with right foot and punches straight out with right fist; left man slidesteps forward and blocks outward with open-hand blow.

652

653. Left man slashes into side of neck with open right hand, palm up.

654. Left man slashes into neck with open left hand, palm up.

* Left man slidesteps back into low fist on-guard; right man steps back into low fist on-guard.

* Return to starting position. (End.)

653   654

655   656

Fourth routine

* Starting position.

* Both men step back with right foot into low fist on-guard.

655. Right man steps forward with right foot and punches straight out with right fist; left man slidesteps forward and blocks outward with inside edge of left forearm, palm toward face.

656. Without arm movement, left man kicks into midsection with right foot.

657. As left man places kicking foot down, he delivers straight punch with right fist, aiming at head.

* Left man slidesteps back into low fist on-guard; right man steps back into low fist on-guard.

* Return to starting position. (End.)

Fifth routine

* Starting position.

* Both men step back with right foot into low fist on-guard.

658 659

658. Right man steps forward with right foot and punches straight out with right fist; left man pivots on left foot to left side and places both hands on ground.

659. Left man delivers high kick with right foot.

* Left man recovers into low fist on-guard; right man steps back into low fist on-guard.

* Return to starting position. (End.)

660   661

Sixth routine

* Starting position.

660. Left man steps back into low fist on-guard; right man steps back into fists at side on-guard, palms up.

661. Right man steps forward with right foot and delivers double fist punch straight out, palms down; left man slidesteps forward and blocks down with both forearms.

662. Left man grips cloth at upper arms with both hands.

663. Left man kicks into face with right knee as he pulls downward with both arms.

* Both men return to stances as in 660.

* Return to starting position. (End.)

662   663

664

Seventh routine

* Starting position.

* Both men step back with right foot into low fist on-guard.

664. Right man attacks (steps forward with right foot and punches straight out with right fist); left man slidesteps forward, parries cross-body with his left forearm.

665. Left man punches low with right fist; right man blocks with left forearm.

666. Right man counters with right punch into face; left man blocks upward with left forearm.

* Left man slidesteps back into low fist on-guard; right man steps back into low fist on-guard.

* Return to starting position. (End.)

In this routine, for the first time we encounter an attack, a counter-attack, and a counter-counterattack.

665   666

Eighth routine

667   668

*   Starting position.

*   Both men step back with right foot into low fist on-guard.

*   Right man attacks; left man slidesteps forward and blocks outward with left forearm.

667.   Left man counters with overhead hammer block to head; right man blocks upward with left forearm.

668.   Right man counters with back-knuckle blow into face; left man blocks upward with left forearm.

*   Left man slidesteps back into low fist on-guard; right man steps back into low fist on-guard.

*   Return to starting position. (End.)

Ninth routine

*   Starting position.

*   Both men step back with right foot into low fist on-guard.

669.   Right man attacks; left man slidesteps forward and blocks outward with left open-hand slash.

670.   Left man grips cloth of blocked right upper arm.

669

670

671. Left man punches with right fist into face as he pulls forward on captured arm; right man blocks upward with left arm.

672. Right man kicks with left foot into midsection; left man blocks down with right forearm.

* Left man slidesteps back into low fist on-guard; right man steps back into low fist on-guard.

* Return to starting position. (End.)

671 **672**

Tenth routine

* Starting position.

* Both men step back with right foot into low fist on-guard.

673. Right man attacks; left man slidesteps forward and catches blow into left palm.

673

674 675

674. Left man grips wrist of punching hand.

675. Left man kicks into midsection with right foot as he pulls captured arm forward; right man blocks down with left forearm.

676. Right man counters with left hooking kick into midsection; left man blocks down with right forearm.

* Left man slidesteps back into low fist on-guard; right man steps back into low fist on-guard.

* Return to starting position. (End.)

676

Eleventh routine

* Starting position.

* Both men step back with right foot into low fist on-guard.

677: Right man attacks with right hooking kick; left man slidesteps forward and blocks outward with left forearm.

677

678. Left man counters with right punch to face; right man blocks upward with left forearm.

679. Right man counters with right fist into face; left man blocks upward with left forearm.

* Left man slidesteps back into low fist on-guard; right man steps back into low fist on-guard.

* Return to starting position. (End.)

678　679

Twelfth routine

* Starting position.

* Both men step back into low fist on-guard.

680　681

680. Right man attacks with right hooking kick; left man slidesteps forward and blocks outward with left forearm.

681. Left man counters with right forward kick; right man blocks with crossed wrist block down.

183

682   683

682. Right man counters with right forward kick; left man blocks down with left forearm.

683. Left man slidesteps back into low fist on-guard; right man steps back into low fist on-guard.

684   685

684. Return to starting position.

685. Bow.

*   Return to starting position. (End.)

TRIPS AND THROWS

The trips and throws used in contest Karate are simpler than throws used in contest Judo. They do not require the same development of technique as Judo throws. Whereas in contest Judo the throw wins the primary point, there is no point given for the throw in contest Karate; the throw serves only to put your opponent into weak position so that a point blow can be delivered. Trips and throws are only allowed for brown and black belt level contest. Purple belt contestants are not permitted to use trips and throws. When the throws and trips are demonstrated for achievement of belt degrees, they are executed in formal style with partners bowing at the start and after the throw is completed.

HOOKING TRIP

* Starting position (the same position as for the routines).

* Bow.

* Return to starting position.

686. Both men step back with right foot into low fist on-guard.

686 687

687. Right man slidesteps forward, attacking with slash (left hand); left man slidesteps forward and blocks upward with left forearm.

688 689

688. With right hand, left man grips cloth at opponent's upper arm, and with left hand grips opponent's wrist. After gripping, he rocks opponent back so that his right foot bears most of his weight.

689. Left man hooks opponent's forward foot at tendon with instep (top of foot) and swings it forward, continuing pushing back motion with arms. It is the combination of foot and arm work which makes the trip successful.

690 691

690. As hooked foot is brought up and opponent's balance is completely lost, left man reverses direction of arm movement, pulling opponent toward him, down, and around.

691. Point is demonstrated by delivering punch (as shown) or kick after opponent is on ground.

*   Both men resume starting position.

SWEEPING TRIP

*   Starting position.

*   Both men step back with right foot into low fist on-guard.

*   Right man slidesteps forward, attacking with left-handed slash; left man slidesteps forward and blocks upward with left forearm.

*   With right hand, left man grips cloth at opponent's upper arm and with left hand grips opponent's wrist. After gripping, he rocks opponent back so that his weight is mainly on right foot.

692. With bottom of right foot, left man sweeps opponent's foot.

*   As swept foot is brought up and opponent's balance is completely broken, left man reverses direction of arm movement, pulling opponent toward him, down, and around.

692

* Left man delivers punch or kick when opponent is on ground.

* Both men resume starting position.

   STRAIGHT FOOT THROW

* Starting position.

* Both men step back with right foot into low fist on-guard.

693. Right man slidesteps forward, attacking with left-handed slash; left man slidesteps forward and brings rear foot up against forward foot; he blocks upward with left forearm and then grips opponent's upper arm with right hand and opponent's wrist with left hand.

694. Left man places extended left leg behind opponent's legs.

693   694
695   696

695. Left man executes throw by first pulling opponent toward him, so that his balance is broken, then down and around.

696. Left man delivers punch or kick when opponent is on ground.

* Both men resume starting position.

INSIDE SWEEPING FOOT THROW

* Starting position.

* Both men step back into low fist on-guard.

* Right man slidesteps forward, attacking with left-handed slash; left man slidesteps forward and blocks upward with left forearm.

* With right hand, left man grips cloth at opponent's upper arm and with left hand grips opponent's wrist; after gripping, he rocks opponent back so that his weight is mainly on right foot.

697   698

697. Left man sweeps opponent's forward foot from inside with bottom of left foot.

698. As the swept foot is brought up and out and opponent's balance is completely broken, left man reverses direction of arm movement, pulling opponent toward him, down, and around.

* Left man delivers punch or kick when opponent is on ground.

* Both men resume starting position.

DOWN ON KNEE BACK TRIP

* Starting position.

* Both men step back into low fist on-guard.

* Right man slidesteps forward, attacking with left slash; left man slidesteps forward and brings rear foot up against forward foot; he blocks upward with left forearm, then grips opponent's upper arm with right hand as he grips opponent's lapel with left hand.

699   700

699. Left man lowers himself onto right knee (his grip on standing man helps to ease him down), placing himself so that his left knee is behind opponent's legs.

700. Left man executes throw by first pulling opponent toward him so that his balance is broken, then down and around.

701. Left man delivers punch when opponent is on ground.

* Both men return to starting position.

701

ADVANCED BROWN BELT FORM (FIRST BROWN BELT)

This is the only formal technique required for the degree of Advanced Brown Belt (First Brown Belt). The other requirement for the achievement of the degree is contest points.

There are 90 moves in this long form. In order to make the movements easier to follow, we have included some photos which show the transition from one position to another. These transitions are indicated by (**A**), following the photo number. There is never a hesitation at the transition position. Unlike the other forms, this one has a combination of fast and slow movements. The fast action is done, as usual, with snap, drive, and force. The slow movements are done with exaggerated precision—flowing, graceful, elegant—yet masculine and strong. Fast actions are indicated by (f) and slow actions by (s), beginning with 723. Before that photo, all actions are fast.

702

703

704

705

702. Starting position.

703. Bow.

704. Return to starting position.

705. Ready stance.

706. Left punch, right step.

707. Right punch, left step.

708. Right step, right block up.

706   707

709. Left step, left block up.

709A. Pivot on ball of left foot counterclockwise to face rear.

710. Right step; right block down.

708   709   709A   710

710A. Pivot on ball of left foot, turn counterclockwise 360 degrees and face rear.

711. At completion of turn, as you place right foot down, right block down.

712. Pivot on ball of left foot, step counterclockwise with right foot to right side; left hand slashes forward.

713. Pivot on ball of right foot, turn clockwise 180 degrees, and step to left side with left foot, right hand slashes forward.

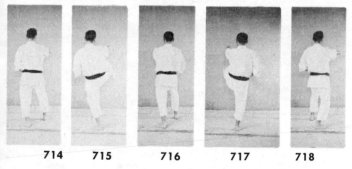

714. Pivot on left foot, turn counterclockwise to face rear, punch with right.

715. Left foot in place, right kick.

716. As right foot is placed down, punch with left.

717. Left foot kick.

718. As left foot is placed down, punch with right.

718A. For this turn, left foot does not step; pivot on ball of left foot and step around counterclockwise, ending to face at a 45 degree left front. Hands are held palm out and make sweeping movement with turn.

719. Hesitate at end of turn.

720. Backhand slash, right hand.

720A. Pivot on right foot, turn clockwise to face right front. Hands make sweeping motion.

718A 719 720 720A

721 722 722A 723

721. Hesitate at end of turn.

722. Backhand slash, left hand.

722A. THIS IS THE FIRST OF THE SLOW MOVEMENTS. Pivot on left foot, turn counterclockwise to face left front.

723. Place right foot forward, extend right fist, bring left fist to side.

724. **724A.** **725.** **726.**

724. This is a complete movement (not transitional) though very slight. Turn to look right front and point right foot to begin pivot (s).

724A. Pivot on ball of right foot, turn clockwise to face right front, left hand extended in slash position (s).

725. Hesitate.

726. Punch out with left (s).

727. **728.** **729.** **729A.**

727. Slight gesture. Begin pivot on left foot, look toward left front (s).

728. Pivot on ball of left foot counterclockwise to face left front. Complete movement with right foot forward, left hand forward in slashing attitude (s).

729. Without stepping, pivot on both feet, turn counterclockwise to face right rear. Hands in raised slashing on-guard (s).

729A. Left foot in place, step with right foot to right rear (s).

| 730 | 731 | 731A | 732 |

730. Complete movement with right foot forward, left hand in slashing position (s).

731. Slight movement. Look to left rear, begin pivot on right foot (s).

731A. Pivot on right foot, stepping clockwise with left foot (s).

732. Complete movement facing left rear, left foot forward, right hand in slashing position.

733. Three simultaneous gestures, slow but definite. Look to right front, pivot left foot, extend arms to side (s).

733A. Pivot on left foot, step around counterclockwise, arms merely follow movement of body (s).

734. Complete movement facing right front, right foot extended, left hand forward (s).

735. Look to right rear, start to pivot right foot (s).

| 733 | 733A | 734 | 735 |

735A **736** **737** **737A**

735A.   Pivot on right foot clockwise.

736.   Complete movement facing right rear, left foot forward, right hand extended in slashing attitude (s).

737.   Look front, pivot left foot (s).

737A.   (Note: Fast movements follow.) Pivot counterclockwise to face front.

738 **739** **740**

738.   As you place foot down to complete turn, execute back-knuckle blow with vigor (f).

739.   Forward high kick, right foot (f); set right foot down forward.

740.   Double arm block outward, elbows in (f).

741. Left hand punches cross body (f); step forward with right foot.

742. Step forward with left foot, punch cross body with right fist (f).

741   742

743   744   745   746   747

743. Step forward with right foot into ready stance (f).

744. Turning clockwise, make 180 degree turn to face rear, blocking down with right arm, right foot forward (f).

745. Step with left foot into ready stance (f).

746. Step with right foot to left rear, block outward with right forearm (f).

747. Left foot in place, take another step out with right foot, punch with left fist (f).

748. Step with left foot to right rear, block outward with left forearm (f).

749. Right foot in place, take another step out with left foot, punch out with right fist.

748 749 750

750. Step out with right foot into ready stance (f).

751. Turn counterclockwise, step with left, pivot on right foot, block down with left arm (f).

752. Step forward with right foot into ready stance (f).

753. (Note: Slow movements follow.) Extend arms, palms down (s).

754. Place right foot lightly forward, toe pointed outward, bearing only slight weight; swing arms into crossed open-hand position (s).

755. Step forward with right foot, hands in slashing on-guard (s).

751 752 753 754 755

756. Place left foot lightly forward, cross open hands (s).

757. Step forward with left foot, hands in slashing on-guard (s).

758. Raise right foot (this is not a kick) (s).

758A. Pivot on left foot (using raised leg as counterweight), turn counterclockwise (s).

759. Complete turn facing rear, place right foot down (s), block down with right arm (f).

760. Step with left foot into ready stance (s).

761. Step with right foot (f), slash with right hand.

762. Pivot on left foot, step counterclockwise to face right side into -ready stance (s).

763. Slash and step to right rear with right hand, right foot (f).

764. Step and slash to right front with left hand, left foot (f).

765. Turn counterclockwise, pivot on left foot to face left side, assume ready stance (s).

766. Step and slash to left rear with left hand and left foot (f).

763   764   765   766

767. Step and slash to left front with right hand and right foot (f).

768. Left foot in place, step and block to front with right hand, right foot (f).

769. Step and block to front with left hand, left foot (f).

770. Step forward with right foot into ready stance (s).

767   768   769   770

771. Pivot on left foot, turn clockwise, step to rear with right foot, block outward with right hand (f).

772. No foot movement. Block downward with right arm (f).

773. Step to rear with left foot, block outward with left arm (f).

774. Block downward with left arm (f).

771   **772**   **773**   **774**

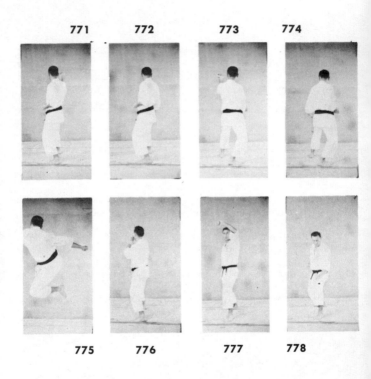

775   **776**   **777**   **778**

775. Leaping side kick, right foot (f). Land with right foot forward.

776. Right elbow blow. Slap right forearm with left hand (f).

777. Without stepping, pivot on both feet, turn counterclockwise to face front, block upward with left arm (f).

778. No foot movement. Block down with left arm (f).

778A. Pivot on left foot, turn counterclockwise 360 degrees (f).

779. At the completion of the turn, squat with left foot forward, slap mat with right hand (f).

780. In continuous motion from 779, spring up, kick forward with right foot (f).

781. Land with right foot forward, crossed-arm block upward (f).

782. Step counterclockwise to face left side, block up with right arm (f).

783. No foot movement. Punch out with left fist (f).

784. Pivot on left foot, step counterclockwise to rear with right foot, block upward with right arm (f).

785. No foot movement. Punch to rear with left fist (f).

786. Pivot on left foot, step counterclockwise to face right side, block upward with right arm (f).

787. No foot movement. Punch out with left fist (f).

788. Right foot in place, step to front with left foot; backhanded knuckle blow with left fist (f).

789. Punch and kick with right hand and foot (f).

* Place right foot back, assume ready stance (s).

* Assume starting position (s).

* Bow.

* Resume starting position. (End.)

786   787   788   789

BLACK BELT FORMS

First form

This is a slow motion form. All moves except one (indicated in the instruction) are executed with exaggerated precision, deliberate hesitation between moves, and flowing, strong gestures. There is nothing feminine about the appearance of this form; it is tiger-like in its grace.

* Starting position.

790. Position of meditation: feet apart, knees slightly bent, head down, hands palm down.

* Return to starting position.

790   **791**   **792**   **793**

* Bow

* Return to starting position.

791. Ready stance.

792. Step forward with right foot, double crossed-arm block, open hands.

793. Outward block with both forearms.

794   **795**   **796**   **797**

794. Slashing block to left front with left hand.

795. Return to ready stance.

796. Left-handed parry, cross-body (pushing motion).

797. Return to ready stance.

798. Slash straight forward with left hand.

799. Return to ready stance.

800. Blocking position as shown. This is a stylized gesture. Imitate photo.

801. Block outward with left hand, palm up.

802. Pushing (parry) gesture cross-body with left hand.

803. (Note that there has been no foot movement since 793.) Step forward with left foot, crossed-arm block upward.

804. Palm up, block outward with right hand.

805. Turn hand over and block outward with right hand.

806. Step forward with right foot, crossed-arm block upward.

807. Open hands, make circular motion with both hands, end with hands touching, palms up.

808. Return fists to ready position.

809. *This is a fast move.* Return to hand position in 807, with quick motion and then return to fist ready position **810.** (In the entire form, this is the only motion accompanied by audible Ki-ya.)

811. Bring open hands together, palms facing each other.

808 809 810 811 812

812. Pushing forward motion with both hands, arms fully extended.

813. Return fists to ready position.

814. Bring open hands together, palms facing.

813 814 815 816 817

815. Step back with right foot, push forward with both hands, arms extended.

816. Bring fists back to ready position.

817. Bring open hands together, palms facing.

818. Step back with left foot as both hands push forward, arms fully extended.

819. Return fists to ready position.

820. Assume stylized blocking hand position.

818   **819**   **820**   **821**

821. Step forward with left foot and assume meditative stance.

*   Return to starting position.

*   Bow.

*   Return to starting position. (End.)

Second form
There are no fast movements in this form.

*   Assume starting position.

822. Assume meditative stance.

*   Return to starting position.

*   Bow.

*   Return to starting position.

823. Step forward with left foot, left hand in fist on-guard.

206

824. Block downward with right forearm.

825. Return to left hand fist on-guard.

826. Punch upward with right fist.

824

827. Return to left fist on-guard.

828. Block downward with left forearm.

829. Block up and outward with left forearm.

825 826 827 828 829

830. Step forward with right foot, assume right fist on-guard.

831. Block down with left forearm.

832. Return to right fist on-guard.

833. Punch upward with left fist.

834. Return to right fist on-guard.

830 831 832 833 834

835. Block down with right forearm.

836. Block up and outward with right forearm.

837. Step forward with left foot, assume left hand slashing on-guard.

838. With left hand, make half a circle with palm away. Direction of the movement is down, out, and up.

839. At finish of movement in 838, assume left slashing on-guard.

840. Block down with left open hand.

841. Parry cross-body with left open hand.

842. Return to left slashing on-guard.

843. Block down with right open hand.

844. Draw right elbow back, then stab straight forward with right open hand.

845. Step forward with right foot and assume right slashing on-guard.

846. Make half-circular movement with left open hand, palm out.

847. At finish of movement in 846, return to right slashing on-guard.

848. Block down with right open hand.

849. Parry cross-body with right open hand.

850. Return to right slashing on-guard.

851. Block down with left open hand.

852. Draw left elbow back, then stab straight forward with left open hand.

853. Return to right slashing on-guard.

854. Place left open hand under right forearm.

855. Extend right hand forward fully, slide left hand up under right arm. Step back with right foot as arm movements are executed.

853   **854**   **855**   **856**   **857**

856. Place right open hand, palm down, beneath left forearm.

857. Step back with left foot, extend left arm fully, slide right hand underneath left arm.

* Meditative position.

* Return to starting position.

* Bow.

* Return to starting position. (End.)

Third form
All movements are in slow motion.

* Assume starting position.

* Assume meditative stance.

* Return to starting position.

* Bow.

* Return to starting position.

858. Extend arms fully to sides, palms down.

858

859. **860.** **861.** **862.**

859. Bring extended arms together, forward, palms facing.

860, 861, 862. Are a continuous movement. Bring arms down to sides, up and outward (describing a full circle), finish movement with arms extended forward.

863. **864.** **865.** **866.**

863. Hesitate.

864. Place right forearm over left, palms down.

865. Assume on-guard toward left front, stepping with left foot.

866. Draw right hand to side as left open hand makes block upward.

867. Slash down with left hand.

868. Resume on-guard.

869. Block down with right hand.

867 868

869 **870** **871** **872**

870. Draw right elbow back.

871. Stab out with right open hand.

872. Resume on-guard.

873. Step forward with right foot to right front. Assume on-guard.

874. Block up with right hand.

875. Block down with right hand.

874 **875**

873

876 877 878 879

876. Resume on-guard.

877. Block down with left hand.

878. Draw left elbow back.

879. Poke straight out with left open hand.

880. Resume on-guard.

880

881. Step front with left foot and assume slashing on-guard.

882. Back of hand parry outward, right hand.

883. Palm of right hand parry, cross-body.

884. Resume slashing on-guard.

881 882 883 884

885. Stab straight forward with right open hand.

886. Resume on-guard.

887. Heel of palm blow upward with right hand.

888. Resume on-guard.

889. Palm-up slash, cross-body, left hand.

890. Turn palm down, then reverse slash.

891. Step forward with right foot, assume slashing on-guard.

892. Backhanded parry, left hand.

893. Palm-of-hand parry, cross-body.

894. Resume on-guard.

895. Stab forward with left open hand.

896. Resume on-guard.

897. Heel-of-palm blow upward, left hand.

898. Resume on-guard.

| 895 | 896 | 897 | 898 |

899. Palm-up slash, cross-body, right hand.

900. Turn palm down, reverse slash.

901. Continue slashing motion of 900 backward, step back with right foot, assume raised arm slashing on-guard.

902. Step back with left foot, reverse arms to raised arm slashing on-guard.

* Assume meditative stance.

* Return to starting position.

* Bow.

* Return to starting position. (End.)

| 899 | 900 | 901 | 902 |

Fourth form

All movements are in slow motion.

* Assume starting position.

* Assume meditative stance.

* Return to starting position.

* Bow.

* Return to starting position.

903   904

903. Ready stance.

904. Left foot in place, point right foot to right side, place hands fist over fist at left side.

905   906   907   908

905. Place right foot at left knee. Hesitate.

906. Extend right leg fully. Hesitate.

907. Place right foot down, as you make back-knuckle blow with right fist, place left palm under right elbow.

908. Without stepping, pivot on both feet to face left side, place fist over fist at right side.

909. Place left foot at right knee. Hesitate.

910. Extend left leg fully. Hesitate.

911. As left foot is placed down, make back-knuckle blow with left fist, place right palm under left elbow.

216

909   910   911

912. Step to front with right foot, place fist over fist at left side.

913. Draw right foot to left knee. Stork stance. Hesitate.

914. Extend right leg fully forward. Hesitate.

915. As right leg is placed down, make backhanded knuckle blow with right fist, place left palm under right elbow.

916. Without stepping, pivot counterclockwise to face rear, fist over fist at right side.

912   913   914   915   916

917. Place left foot at right knee. Hesitate.

917

918   919   919A   920   921

918. Extend left leg fully. Hesitate.

919. As left foot is placed down, make backhanded knuckle blow with left fist, placing right palm under left elbow.

919A. Pivot on left foot, swinging right foot around counterclockwise to make 180 degree turn.

920. At finish of turn, place right foot forward, assume fist on-guard.

* Stork stance. Hesitate.

921. Make low kick forward with ball of right foot as you punch down with right fist. Hesitate.

* Return to stork stance.

922. Kick to right front, low, with edge of right foot as you make edge of fist blow with right hand. Hesitate.

* Return to stork stance.

923. Kick to left front with inside edge of right foot, as you punch downward with heel of closed hand.

922

923

*   Return to stork stance.

924.   Right fist on-guard.

925.   Pivot on both feet, turn counterclockwise to face rear, assume left fist on-guard.

*   Facing rear, repeat movements as in 920 to 924, end with left fist on-guard.

924   **925**   **926**   **927**   **928**

926.   Without stepping, pivot left foot, pointing toe to 45 degrees, shift body slightly (counterclockwise).

927.   Hook kick to rear with right foot. Hesitate.

928.   Left foot in place, put right foot down on mat (toe pointing right), fists palm-over-palm at right side.

929.   Hook kick to front with left foot.

930.   Return to ready stance.

*   Return to starting position.

*   Bow.

*   Return to starting position. (End.)

   Fifth form
All movements are in slow motion.

*   Starting position.

*   Position of meditation.

929   **930**

219

931 **932**

* Return to starting position.

* Bow.

* Return to starting position.

931. Ready stance with forearms extended, fists held palm up.

932. Feet in place, double-handed slash to right using sweeping gesture.

* Return to extended forearm ready stance, as in 931.

933 **934** **935** **936**

933. Double-handed slash to left, sweeping gesture.

* Return to extended forearm ready stance.

934. Draw right leg up, hesitate.

935. Extend right leg to right side.

936. Place right foot behind left foot, cross-legged, knees slightly bent.

937. Draw left leg up, hesitate.

937

938   **939**   **940**   **941**

938.   Extend left leg to left side.

939.   Place left foot down so that toe points to rear, while right toe continues to point front.

940.   Pivot on left foot, turn to rear, place both hands on mat.

941.   Kick up with right foot.

941A.   Push up with hands, swing right leg counterclockwise.

942.   Continuation of this brings you facing front in standard ready stance. Right foot does not touch mat until turn is completed.

943.   Ceremonial fighting stance, left hand and foot forward.

944.   Draw left foot to right knee.

945.   Kick forward with left foot.

941A   **942**   **943**   **944**   **945**

    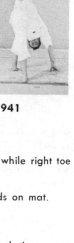

946. Place left foot down forward, right hand slash block up to right.

947. Left open hand stab forward, draw right open hand to right side.

948. Step forward with right foot into ceremonial fighting stance, right hand forward.

949. Draw right foot to left knee.

950. Kick forward with right foot.

951. Place right foot down forward, left hand slashing block up to left.

952. Right open hand stab forward, draw left open hand to left side.

953. Pivot on both feet counterclockwise to face rear. As turn is made, raise right hand in slashing on-guard, left open hand under right elbow, palm down.

954. Draw left foot to right knee.

955. Kick to rear with left foot. Hesitate.

956. Place left foot down, point toe to side, shifting hands to reverse position shown in 953.

957. Draw right leg up.

958. Hook kick with right leg.

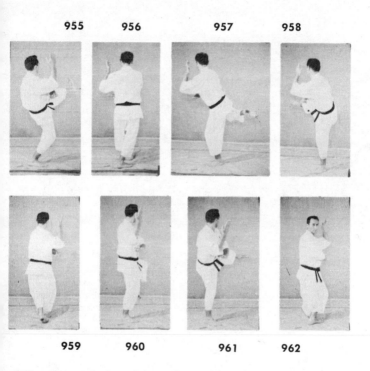

955   956   957   958

959   960   961   962

959. Place right foot down in front of left foot, point toe to side. Place foot down, switch hands to return to position in 953.

960. Draw left leg up to right knee.

961. Side snap kick toward rear with left leg.

962. Right foot in place, put left foot down in front of right foot as body turns to face front. Place foot down, shift hands to reverse position.

963. Draw right foot up to left knee.

964. Kick toward front with right foot.

965. Place right foot down to assume ready stance as fists are placed at sides.

*   Starting position.

*   Bow.

*   Starting position. (End.)

963

964

965